The

Victorian
Home

The
Victorian
Home

THE GRANDEUR AND COMFORTS
OF THE VICTORIAN ERA,
IN HOUSEHOLDS PAST AND PRESENT

Ellen M. Plante

COURAGE
BOOKS

AN IMPRINT OF RUNNING PRESS
PHILADELPHIA • LONDON

9 8 7 6 5 4 3

Digit on the right indicates the number of this printing.

Library of Congress Cataloging-in-Publication Number 94-74909

ISBN 0-7624-0390-X

THE VICTORIAN HOME
The Grandeur and Comforts of the Victorian Era,
in Households Past and Present
was prepared and produced by
Michael Friedman Publishing Group, Inc.
15 West 26th Street
New York, New York 10010

Editor: Susan Lauzau
Art Director: Jeff Batzli
Designer: Lynne Yeamans
Photography Editor: Jennifer Crowe McMichael

Color separations by Bright Arts (Singapore) Pte. Ltd.
Printed in China by Leefung-Asco Printers Ltd.

This book may be ordered by mail from the publisher.
Please add $2.50 for postage and handling.
But try your bookstore first!

Courage Books, an imprint of
Running Press Book Publishers
125 South Twenty-second Street
Philadelphia, Pennsylvania 19103-4399

Dedication

To all who are Victorian spirits at heart

Acknowledgments

Special thanks to Kelly Matthews of Michael Friedman Publishing Group, Inc.,

for the opportunity to complete this text and the immense pleasure derived from

same; to my lifelong friend Rita Halliday, who assumed the task of typing my manuscript

and did a superb job; to Carolyn Flaherty, my editor at Victorian Homes magazine, who

invited me to become a member of the VH family several years ago and introduced

my column, "Collecting Victoriana"; and to my husband and children, who are always

supportive despite the ever-growing mounds of books and papers that seem to take

over our small nineteenth-century home.

C O N T E N T S

Introduction

———

Victorian decorating, today a full-fledged style born of the Victorian Revival during the 1980s, is perhaps the most inspired way of turning a house into "home."

———

Victorians carefully designed their homes to create a look of comfort and opulence. The home was the center of the universe for the Victorian family, a safe haven from a rapidly industrializing society. As such, home was a blending of rooms in which to entertain, gather the family, or steal a moment of quiet repose. Each room was painstakingly decorated according to the purpose it served; the ornate parlor and the well-dressed dining room conveyed to guests an impression of wealth, power, and high social standing.

———

To fully appreciate Victorian style and to bring Victoriana into the home of the 1990s—whether a gloriously restored Queen Anne, a cozy cottage, a suburban tract house, or an apartment—a closer look at the decorating trends and furnishings popular throughout the nineteenth century is called for.

———

Victorian spirit is everywhere apparent in this cozy corner bedecked with cabbage roses on walls and fabric. A bamboo étagère plays host to cherished collectibles, while the wicker chaise longue speaks of stylish comfort. Candlelight and fresh flowers add the perfect finishing touch in this romantic setting.

The Early Victorian Period

FURNITURE STYLES

When we speak of the Victorian period, we are recalling the period from 1837 to 1901, when Queen Victoria reigned over Great Britain and its growing empire. Over the years, various furnishings and nineteenth-century accessories have been generically referred to as Victorian, but there are in fact several distinct styles that predominated throughout the Victorian era.

Between the 1830s and the 1860s several revival styles influenced furniture design. As Queen Victoria took the throne in the late 1830s, many homes in the United States were outfitted with American Empire furnishings, which coincided with the debut of Greek Revival architecture. These massive pieces, usually constructed of cherry or mahogany, displayed subtle rectangular lines. They were somewhat plain, yet elegant when adorned with gilt stenciling or impressive paw feet.

As architects and craftsmen looked to the past for inspiration, the mystery of the middle ages combined with romanticism to produce a Gothic Revival. Victorian homes were built in the Gothic style with eye-catching arched windows reminiscent of French cathedrals, and the rosewood and oak furnishings produced between 1840 and 1860 were easily recognized by their Gothic arches, spool turnings, and carved trefoils (ornamental embellishments resembling a threefold leaf such as the clover).

Rococo Revival furniture was being produced between 1850 and 1870, and this style,

"How to Build a Happy Home—Six things are requisite. Integrity must be the architect, tidiness the upholsterer. It must be warmed by affection, lighted up with cheerfulness; and industry must be the ventilator, renewing the atmosphere, and bringing in fresh salubrity day by day; while over all, as a protecting canopy and glory, nothing will suffice except the blessing of God."

Godey's Lady's Book,
August 1855

Careful attention to detail, from the floral wall-paper frieze to the elegant drapery puddling at the floor, creates a perfect backdrop for period furnishings in this High Style corner. The beautiful Rococo Revival armchair features a carved crest and lush, red upholstery with button tufting.

recalling eighteenth-century France, brought delicate upholstered furnishings crafted from rosewood or black walnut into Victorian parlors. These serpentine pieces were elegantly dressed with carved fruits, flowers, birds, vines, or tendrils. Accessories such as gilded mirrors and delicate marble-top tables completed the setting.

A familiar name associated with the Rococo Revival style is John Henry Belter, a New York cabinetmaker who turned out exceptional furnishings with striking architectural embellishments, ornamentations, and veneered burled-walnut panels. While Belter was handcrafting his exquisite pieces, factories were mass-producing the ever-popular parlor sets, which were made well into the 1860s.

Considered a Rococo Revival substyle, cast-iron furniture and accessories for the home and garden were also produced during the 1850s and 1860s. Hat racks, garden chairs, benches, and stools were usually painted white, and most were decorated with the same fruit and floral motifs found on wooden furniture from the same period.

In sharp contrast to the graceful Rococo Revival style, the Renaissance Revival in furniture design brought large pieces into vogue between the 1860s and the 1880s. Generally crafted of sturdy walnut, French-inspired Renaissance Revival pieces took center stage with their carved or applied ornamentation, such as medallions, pediments, scrolls, and fruitwood pulls.

While these early-Victorian-period revival styles were often introduced via the cabinetmaker's shop, the Industrial Revolution, well under way by the mid-nineteenth century, allowed for the production of machine-made furniture in the various styles. As a result, the aspiring middle class as well

furniture became a popular alternative to more costly or formal styles—especially in the bedroom. Softwoods such as pine, poplar, and birch were used in construction; the furniture was then painted in light or pastel shades of pink, blue, green, lavender, gray, or white. Women and children hand-decorated cottage-style furniture with floral designs, imitative graining, stenciled stripes, and so on. Furniture manufacturers found a receptive market among middle-class families furnishing small homes and the well-to-do who had summer residences. As a result, charming pieces such as cottage-style beds, dressers, washstands, and desks were manufactured from 1840 through the end of the nineteenth century.

INTERIOR DESIGN

In decorating the home during the early Victorian period, wallpapers and hand-mixed paints were used on interior walls, and color was determined by the purpose of the room. For example, the parlor, the most elegant room in the house, was to be painted in light shades to avoid being dreary during the evening. Various shades of pink, gray, and green were commonly used and the woodwork was generally painted a darker tint of the same color.

By the 1850s, architects and noted publications such as *Godey's Lady's Book* (a monthly that was introduced in 1830) were routinely discussing color theory, and new recommendations encouraged women to have their rooms painted in either harmonizing or contrasting colors: shades such as violet, peach, salmon, sage, and brownstone were frequently used in "dressing" the wall in a harmonizing scheme, while more vibrant hues such as crimson and green were

as the nouveau riche had access to the latest fashions in home decoration. As different styles appeared, and then disappeared just as suddenly, many of them overlapped. Homes were often a tasteful mixture of furniture styles rather than a series of rooms decked out in a singular fashion. For example, when Andrew Jackson Downing wrote *Cottage Residences* in 1842, his book was illustrated with gaily painted furniture and spool-turned beds and tables. Affordable and designed to appeal to the working class, "cottage-style"

Interior design during the early Victorian period combined decorative touches such as this small-patterned wallpaper treatment, simple window dressing, and wall-to-wall carpet. Placement of the furniture around walls rather than in intimate groupings was also preferred early in the era.

employed in a contrasting finish. Baseboards and moldings were either painted or "grained" in imitation of elegant woods.

After the introduction of machine-made wallpaper in the 1840s, middle-class Victorian homeowners were papering parlors and bedrooms with zeal. Early patterns included landscape scenes; nature scenes; historical papers featuring prominent figures; architectural papers, which gave the room added embellishments; ashlar papers, which imitated stone; and flocked or "velvet" papers, which gave the appearance of damask fabric. Striped papers and wallpapers with small, overall designs were also used, especially in bedrooms.

Trends in wallpaper design did not change as quickly as styles in paint colors, and throughout the mid-century period, scenic papers, papers that imitated wood grain, papers with small geometric patterns, and architectural papers remained in use.

Floors in the early Victorian period were either painted or covered with a floorcloth, matting, or wall-to-wall carpet. As carpeting became more affordable during the 1850s, many households began to consider it a necessity for a proper parlor rather than simply another decorative feature.

During the 1830s and 1840s, windows were outfitted with shutters, venetian blinds, fabric roller blinds (window shades), or a simple treatment with two curtains and perhaps a valance.

By 1850, window dressing was becoming an art form, and although interior shutters and blinds were still in use, many middle-class parlors now sported windows with layers including a shade; a "glass curtain," or undercurtain, next to the window; a valance; and ornate drapery made of velvet, brocade, or cotton damask.

> *"Having duly arranged for the physical necessities of a healthful and comfortable home, we next approach the important subject of beauty in reference to the decoration of houses. For while the aesthetic element must be subordinate to the requirements of physical existence...it yet holds a place of great significance among the influences which make home happy and attractive, which give it a constant and wholesome power over the young, and contributes much to the education of the entire household in refinement, intellectual development, and moral sensibility."*
>
> Catharine E. Beecher & Harriet Beecher Stowe
> The American Woman's Home,
> 1869

The Late Victorian Period

FURNITURE STYLES

The tide had turned by the late 1860s as design reformers grew tired of French Revival styles, poorly made factory furnishings, and excessive ornamentation. The most noted reformer, Charles Eastlake, wrote a book entitled *Hints on Household Taste in Furniture, Upholstery and Other Details*, published in England in 1868 and in circulation in America by 1872. In it, he called for the use of simple, well-crafted furnishings in the home and overall changes in interior design. Eastlake's recommendations were well received both in England and in the United States, and greatly influenced home decoration for the next twenty years.

Eastlake-style furnishings, popular in America between 1870 and 1890, were not the handmade, simplistic pieces with medieval or Gothic overtones that the reformer had designed, but rather subdued, rectangular furnishings with fewer embellishments than previous revival styles. Factory-made American Eastlake furniture was usually constructed of cherry, walnut, oak, or oak "look-alikes" such as ash or chestnut. This style is easily recognized by its modest size and its decorative elements such as incised lines, carved geometric patterns, and brass drawer pulls.

"Japanesque" designs and exotic accessories were in vogue from the late 1870s through the turn of the century. The 1876 Centennial Exhibition in Philadelphia (with numerous exhibits devoted to foreign cultures), combined with a love of travel, inspired in the Victorians a desire to evoke a sense of the exotic in their surroundings. Souvenirs were proudly displayed, and suddenly, Japanese-inspired screens, fans, and furnishings, particularly wicker with Oriental designs, appeared throughout the house, most noticeably in the parlor. In addition, Oriental fabrics, tufted pillows, and Turkish chairs were introduced for comfort as well as for a hint of worldliness.

Decorative arts were the focus of the 1880s Aesthetic Movement, which was born of Eastlake's Reform Movement, the British Arts and Crafts Movement, and the late Victorian obsession with exotic cultures. This movement, embracing a study of beauty and a philosophy of art and its various forms, found peacock feathers being used as decorative elements and nature-inspired bamboo furniture strategically placed throughout Victorian rooms.

Following closely on the heels of the Aesthetic Movement, Art Nouveau was influential in accessorizing the Victorian home with realistic interpretations of romantic designs such as floral motifs, flowing swirls, and sensuous curves. Art Nouveau's expressive, nature-inspired style lasted from the early 1890s until after the turn of the century. Wallpaper, glassware, and numerous other items were decorated in this fashion, but perhaps the best-known example of this style can be found in the glasswork of Louis Comfort Tiffany.

The late-nineteenth-century interest in nature and art in a variety of forms found Victorians devoting time and attention to their gardens, and front porches or piazzas became an extended living space. To furnish this outdoor area, wicker proved ideal since it was both sturdy and weather resistant. Made of rattan, reed, willow, or cane, wicker

> *"To fulfil the first and most*
>
> *essential principles of good design,*
>
> *every article of furniture*
>
> *should, at the first glance, proclaim*
>
> *its real purpose..."*
>
> *Charles L. Eastlake*
> Hints on Household Taste, *Fourth (Revised) Edition, 1878*

had been used sporadically since the 1860s, but toward the end of the century it was especially popular. Constructed with curlicues and creative embellishments during the 1880s and 1890s, wicker was found suitable for use indoors as well as on the porch. Everything from bedroom sets to chairs, rockers, tables, and children's furniture was produced in wicker and proudly put to use in the late Victorian period.

During the 1890s, at a time when the Arts and Crafts Movement was making headway in America, wicker began to appear in simplified forms with rectangular shapes and a close-weave design. Eventually open-weave designs were favored as a cost-cutting measure, and after 1900 a great deal of wicker sported this design.

The Arts and Crafts Movement, which began in England in the 1860s and was inspired by the decorative designs of philosopher William Morris and the writings of John Ruskin, made its way to America by

the 1890s. A philosophy based on harmonious union of art and craftsmanship, the movement was pioneered in the United States by American Gustav Stickley. His shop turned out furniture of quality with simple, plain lines. Others followed suit, including Elbert Hubbard, who founded the Roycroft community in East Aurora, New York, where the Roycrofters turned out handcrafted oak furnishings and metalwork.

While these proponents of the Arts and Crafts Movement were applauded for their craftsmanship and lofty ideals, Victorians began to tire of the dark oak and severe lines of the style. Again the experts looked to a revival—specifically the Colonial Revival, which reintroduced early American furniture designs such as Queen Anne and Chippendale after the dawn of the twentieth century.

One last aspect of Victorian furnishings that deserves attention is the introduction of mail-order catalogs in the 1870s and 1880s. All across America and especially throughout the middle states and rural areas, Victorians could purchase the latest in furniture via catalog. Whether it was wicker, brass or iron beds, Arts and Crafts–style pieces, or the golden oak furniture that was popular from 1880 through the turn of the century, a home could be completely outfitted by turning the pages of Montgomery Ward's or Sears, Roebuck and Company's catalog.

Chamber sets for the bedroom, pedestal tables and chairs for the dining room, hall-trees, desks, kitchen cupboards, and parlor sets as well as accessories in the latest fashion were readily available, affordable, and could be delivered to the nearest railroad station and then home. For the first time in history working-class families could savor the household luxuries that had long been enjoyed by the wealthy.

INTERIOR DESIGN

The reform movements that were well under way by the 1870s influenced not only furniture styles but, perhaps more importantly, Victorian interior design.

The Civil War had ended, the country was experiencing unprecedented industrial and economic growth, and as the rich

Inspired by reform movements, these rich wood tones, Oriental rugs, art-glass windows, handsome wainscoting, and antique furnishings work together to create a warm, comfortable setting.

became richer the middle class was growing. With cash in hand, Victorians had the wherewithal to dress their homes in the latest fashion and to lavish attention on even the most minute detail.

When Charles Eastlake wrote *Hints on Household Taste*, he advised a reform in wall treatments. A radical departure from the

early practice of papering entire walls (or painting them) in a single pattern or color, the method Eastlake recommended used wainscoting throughout the house for heightened visual pleasure. Dividing the walls into three separate areas to be decorated became known as the tripartite wall, and included wainscoting or dado—the decorated lower wall—on the bottom portion, followed by a "field," or the large expanse in the middle of the wall, and finally the frieze at the very top. Household design experts sought creative ways to outfit the tripartite wall. Factory-produced wainscot was one alternative, but the use of a chair rail around the room with walls painted or papered above and below the rail was also acceptable. The most popular treatment, however, was created by using different wallpapers to enhance the horizontal division of the wall. During the 1870s and 1880s this was the prevailing fashion in the Victorian parlor, and the effect was carried into other rooms as well.

By the 1890s the tripartite wall treatment had become passé, and Victorians began to simplify their interiors, following the dictates of the Arts and Crafts Movement. A two-part wall treatment, usually a paper and a frieze, was now preferred, or walls were covered with a one-color paper.

Interior walls that were painted during the 1870s and 1880s reflected the taste for tertiary colors such as olive, terra-cotta, plum, claret, citron, and peacock blue. Primary colors were considered garish and the pale shades associated with earlier decades hopelessly old-fashioned.

During the 1890s, colors such as red, yellow, blue, orange, violet, and green were back in style but used with restraint in decorating any one room as "less is more" became a common motto.

Nothing was left to chance in outfitting the Victorian home—even the enclosed porch was dressed in the latest style. Wicker chairs, layers of romantic lace tablecloths, and lush greenery provide the perfect setting for an intimate meal. Add choice antique glassware or ceramics, along with fresh fruit and flowers, for a look that says "welcome."

"In furnishing a house let your guiding rules be that the same style, with modifications, be apparent all over your house, that in the employment of colour you avoid bad contrasts, that walls be well covered with mirrors, pictures, etc., and that the rooms be not overcrowded."

Alexander V. Hamilton
The Household
Cyclopaedia of Practical Receipts
and Daily Wants, *1873*

The wall-to-wall carpeting with large floral or geometric designs prevalent in the early Victorian home was discarded during the last quarter of the nineteenth century in favor of hardwood or parquet flooring with Oriental rugs. Room-size carpets were acceptable if they had a border to add visual impact and break the monotony of such a large expanse. This trend continued until 1900 with variations in color and design.

Window treatments during the late Victorian period became less fussy after Eastlake called for simplicity in window dressings, though the practice of layering continued. Interior shutters painted to match the room were used, as were fabric shades. Lace curtains had come into vogue, and while they were acceptable as a covering during the warmer months, a heavier drapery was still put back up in autumn.

During the 1890s, rod-pocket panels of lace often replaced the window shade. Pleated valances, pinch-pleats, and fringe valances were devised, as were elaborate swags and cascades. Window dressing was open to wide interpretation during the last decade of the century—as was interior design in general—and in contrast to the plainer styles of the reform movements, windows seemed to receive an extraordinary amount of attention and detail in the form of artistic grillwork, fringes, and tassels.

An architectural embellishment known as art glass (also called stained glass) was introduced during the late 1800s, and Victorian homes showed off these eye-catching windows in front doors, bathrooms, stairways, and dining rooms. Beveled glass and etched glass windows, a bit more reserved but striking nonetheless, turned up in Colonial Revival architecture at the turn of the century.

> *"The choice of a wallpaper should be guided in every respect by the destination of the room in which it will be used. The most important question will always be whether it is to form a decoration in itself, or whether it is to become a mere background for pictures."*
>
> *Charles L. Eastlake*
> Hints on Household Taste,
> *Fourth (Revised) Edition, 1878*

Victorian Style in Today's Home

Fortunately for us, the nineteenth century gave rise to so many and such varied styles that today we can choose from a potpourri of Victorian-inspired designs and furnishings in decorating our homes.

We'll explore here the decorating possibilities that predominated during the late Victorian period (circa 1870–1900)—a time of great excitement, social change, and material wealth, and an era in which new heights of interior decoration were achieved. No corner was left bare, no wall unadorned.

Personal mementos and favorite keepsakes were on display; "homeyness" was paramount in each and every room, and artistic liberties created breathtaking settings.

Adapting the style of the late Victorian period for modern-day homes does not, how-

---

Victorian charm pervades this modern country setting in subtle ways. Note the wicker settee dressed with pillows, the wall sconce with glass shades, and the treasured items on display. In true Victorian spirit, architectural details like the triangular window set above French doors also command attention.

ever, preclude the use of Rococo Revival or Renaissance Revival styles, as these furnishings were commonplace well into the 1880s and can serve to anchor a contemporary Victorian setting.

Today's Victorian style, which is explored room by beautiful room throughout this book, can evoke Victoriana in full flower, as well as more subtle touches that convey turn-of-the-century warmth and charm. Personal choice dictates profuse or scaled-down ornamentation: High Style calls to mind the fashionable urban parlor or the romantic sitting room with Oriental flair. In contrast, subtler Victorian influences can be found in the beauty of an Arts and Crafts–inspired room, a comfortable cottage filled with airy wicker, or even a modern or eclectic setting where a singular piece such

as an Art Nouveau lamp or an Eastlake desk imparts nineteenth-century spirit.

As a decorating guide, *The Victorian Home* will introduce you to each room in the house and uncover the history of the room—its purpose as well as its importance for the Victorian family. We'll look at High Style and at touches of Victoriana in furnishings, wall and floor treatments, window dressing, and decorative accessories. Each chapter includes suggestions for personalizing your home with nineteenth-century antiques and collectibles. A source directory is included at the end of the book to help you find the perfect wallpaper, that long-sought lighting fixture, curtains that fit your style, or the ideal antique or reproduction furnishings.

> *"There is nothing cheaper, there is nothing more beautiful, there is nothing that makes a house more cheerful than flowers. They are ready and willing to smile in beauty and loveliness on all who will cultivate their acquaintance and give them hospitality."*
>
> *Richard A. Wells, A.M.*
> Manners, Culture and Dress of the
> Best American Society, *1891*

Today's Victorian Revival in interior design interprets the past with an eye on the present. The wall treatment in this dining room combines a bold use of color with a decorative chair rail. In typical Victorian fashion, a floral area rug dresses a rich hardwood floor, and a soft fabric shade filters light over the table.

A final word: Victorian style is as fitting today as it was a century ago. The overwhelming success of the Victorian Revival during the 1980s points to a common bond uniting us with the Victorians across the span of a hundred years. We face the dawn of a new century, with both anticipation and trepidation, just as the Victorians did. We've returned to our homes to seek comfort and refuge from a fast-paced world and discovered what the Victorians knew all along—home is where the heart is.

CHAPTER ONE

The Proper Parlor

The parlor invokes quintessential Victorian style—both past and present. No other room in the house was the focus of such concentrated efforts with regard to decorating. The proper parlor, given more than just a passing glance, spoke volumes about the Victorian mistress and her family. The smallest object, proudly displayed, could send strong messages in an era marked by symbolic gestures and a strict code of etiquette. A study in contrasts, the Victorian parlor provided an opportunity for the family to show itself to advantage and at the same time was a canvas on which the free spirit held in check by polite society could paint. Liberties could be taken in decorating the parlor; self-expression was evident.

Enter the Victorian parlor, share its history, savor the ideas for creating a Victorian oasis all your own, and delight in the nineteenth-century whimsies that are a hallmark of Victorian style.

The Victorian parlor—the design masterpiece of the nineteenth-century home—conveyed social standing and an appreciation of culture. Opulent, upholstered furnishings, fine artwork, notable architectural details, and elegant touches such as fringed pillows and an ornate tea service combine to pay tribute to the Gilded Age.

The History of the Victorian Parlor

Just as furniture and interior styles went through numerous changes during the Victorian period, so did architectural design. Depending upon the style and size of the house and whether it was suited to a rural or urban area, the late-nineteenth-century home may have had a parlor, a sitting room, a "living room," or some combination of the above.

When Palliser, Palliser & Company made available their plan book, *Palliser's American Cottage Homes,* in 1878, their varied architectural plans continued the trend of assigning a sitting room or living room to smaller family homes, while more elaborate structures such as brownstones and city houses included a formal parlor for entertaining guests as well as a sitting room for family use. Usually located at the front of the residence, the parlor was often separated from the more casual sitting room by wooden pocket doors or by the front hall.

Deportment and ceremony associated with Victorian daily life often played themselves out in the parlor. In an age before the telephone, polite society paid calls, visiting each other's homes to offer congratulations, condolences, or get-well wishes. Such calls, often referred to as "morning calls," were made between noon and 5 P.M., but special care was taken to avoid arriving during a lady's luncheon. Morning calls were typically half an hour or less in duration. In contrast, friendly calls or evening calls among the well acquainted were less formal and could be longer. An evening call was never to commence after 9 P.M., as the caller risked disturbing the family if they had retired early.

The piano used for entertaining in the Victorian parlor also sent an unspoken message that the master of the house was a man of considerable means and the mistress was musically accomplished. Here, the center table set for tea, the elaborate mirror above the mantel, and the tasseled scarf and books atop the piano all speak of good taste.

When paying a call, visitors were greeted at the front door by a domestic servant who accepted a calling card to present to the mistress of the house, and if she was not "engaged," the caller was shown to the parlor. While waiting for the hostess, it was considered improper for a guest to walk about the room examining pictures or bric-a-brac, touch an open piano, or play with a parasol or cane. Victorians nevertheless conducted a visual inspection of their surroundings: a tapestry hung on the wall told them their hostess and her family appreciated travel and the arts, and a few strategically placed books nodded toward intellect and refinement.

Whether the household was humble or grand, the hostess was obliged to make her guests welcome. Lady callers were invited to sit on the sofa or in a chair close to the warmth of the fire during cooler months. A gentleman caller was never to position himself on a sofa next to a lady unless specifically instructed to do so, and it was customary for him to hold his top hat and gloves firmly in his hands during the course of a visit.

The hostess engaged her callers in pleasant conversation; political, religious, or controversial subjects were taboo. It was not necessary for her to serve refreshments during a call, as tea and cakes were reserved for planned afternoon receptions. If the lady of the house happened to be engaged in needlework when a friendly caller arrived, it was acceptable for her to continue her embroidery or crocheting during a visit, as it did not impede her ability to converse, and in fact made her appear enterprising. At the end of a call, the hostess escorted her guest to the door or had a servant do so.

When a dinner party was planned, the guests, usually six to ten in number, gathered in the parlor before being led into the dining room when dinner was announced. While it

---

Victorian influence adds visual impact in this parlor via an elaborate, wall-hung tapestry. Softer touches, such as a draped parlor table and a gold-framed mirror reminiscent of a pier glass placed between two windows, hint at nineteenth-century style.

centrate), perform readings from Shakespeare, play charades, or participate in a theatrical performance. In homes with a connected front and back parlor, pocket doors were opened and the rear parlor or sitting room could serve as a stage for a popular *tableaux vivant*, in which a song or poem was acted out in pantomime.

The parlor was also the setting for weddings, receptions, and family funerals.

Parlors varied in their ornamentation, furnishings, and extravagance, but predominant fashions and styles dictated some similarities in all. The proper parlor was always the best-dressed room in the house, given the scope of its function as a room in which to entertain and receive guests. It was generally reserved for such social occasions unless, of course, it was the only parlor or sitting room. If that was the case, especially in small homes or rural areas, the parlor also functioned as a place for the family to gather.

Depending upon the size of the parlor, furniture was arranged in several intimate groupings. Until the early 1870s, experts suggested that furniture be of a similar style, but before the end of the decade they were calling for a harmonious mixture where no two pieces matched. Early on, parlor sets

had been customary during the mid-nineteenth century for women to retire to the parlor after dinner while men adjourned to the library or remained at the table, conventional practice during the late Victorian period found both men and women retiring to the parlor for conversation or light entertainment. For example, during the autumn and winter months dinner guests might play the popular card game called whist (so called because it required players to be silent and con-

In typical late Victorian fashion, the furniture in this living room or parlor is arranged in several groupings. Seating is provided around the center table for refreshments or amusements; there is an area for intimate conversation; and a chair close to the warmth of a fire offers a cozy spot to read or relax.

were quite popular and usually consisted of a sofa, with or without a love seat, matching armchairs, and a lady's chair or two constructed without arms to accommodate the masses of material that flowed from the latest fashions in dress. While the well-to-do could afford to furnish their homes via the cabinetmaker's shop, the majority of middle-class Victorians purchased the more affordable factory-made sets or individual items.

Literally filling every corner of the room, corner chairs were a frequent addition to the parlor as was an étagère, a tall corner stand for displaying favorite objects. The magnificent étagère was often the most flamboyant furnishing in the room.

To accompany the numerous chairs, tapestry or needlework footstools were scattered about to provide additional comfort, and a generously stuffed ottoman or two, turned with buttons and embellished with fringe, was considered necessary to display an appreciation of the exotic.

If the parlor appeared to overflow with seating possibilities, they were balanced by a like number of tables. A sofa table, lamp tables (called pillar tables), and a large center table were equally important in outfitting this room. The center table, depending upon style, was round, oval, or rectangular, and revival-style examples often sported elegant marble tops. This table could be placed in the middle of the room in order to display favorite objects, or it could be situated more discreetly along a wall.

The majority of parlors boasted a fireplace, the most ornate one in the house, dressed with tile inserts or detailed, carved woodwork. The fireplace not only served to warm a chilly room and cast a romantic, glowing light, but the mantel proved an ideal display area for mementos, photographs, or

Above: The fireplace in this Victorian parlor is accessorized with a floral-patterned fire screen, which is functional as well as decorative. A family portrait presides over the romantic beauty of this gathering place, with its rich velvets, High Style ceiling treatment, and stunning chandelier.

Opposite: Architectural details such as an ornately carved fireplace and elaborate ceiling convey Victorian splendor. The shell of the room was—and still is—eminently important when decorating in the Victorian style. Such a magnificent background deserves equally lavish appointments: candelabra on the mantel, delicate pier tables, and an elegant chandelier complete the High Style adornments.

candlesticks. A fire screen sat close by the hearth to direct heat, but this too was a fancy touch, with an elaborate frame and a canvas featuring needlework or a scene inspired by nature. During those months when the fireplace was not in use, a large bouquet of flowers might be placed in front of the hearth.

Sumptuous window dressings in layers, vibrant Oriental rugs, and soft lighting from a profusion of table lamps added color and pattern to an increasingly eclectic setting and cast a gentle radiance on intimate corners. Stunning walls of beautiful color or choice wallpapers were decorative in and of themselves, and tied the room together in a harmonious blend.

With distinctly feminine frills, both the parlor in full regalia and the parlor with more subtle charms were finished off with an assortment of accessories. Fringed shawls were draped over a chair or two; decorative objects of glass and porcelain graced the table tops; paintings and craftwork items, like picture frames made of seashells, lent a personal touch; and crocheted antimacassars were carefully placed on furnishings to protect the fabric on arm- and headrests.

Liberties could be taken in decorating the parlor during the last few decades of the nineteenth century, and this all-important room began to reflect personal taste and artistic sensibilities rather than a strict doctrine of what was considered acceptable. As new styles emerged a dash of the exotic or a hint of Art Nouveau was introduced into the parlor setting, or a bold stance was taken and a parlor might appear to have stepped out of another time and place.

Not until this past decade, with the emergence of Victorian Revival style, have we had the pleasure of sharing in—and actually living in—such glorious rooms.

Creating a Proper Victorian Parlor

Limited only by the scope of our imaginations, we have the means of creating Victorian grandeur in the 1990s. A style evoking romanticism, daring, personality, excitement, and charm is ours for the taking—in greater or lesser degrees.

Today there are a variety of companies, small businesses, and antiques shops that specialize in architectural woodwork and salvage, floor coverings, paints and wallpapers, lighting fixtures, fabrics, curtains, needlework, and vintage furnishings as well as reproduction furniture designed for the Victorian-inspired home. The source directory included in this book was compiled with the do-it-yourself approach in mind and will provide you with innumerable leads for everything needed to create a Victorian parlor, whether you opt for a full High Style treatment or the lighter touches that evoke just a hint of Victoriana.

High Style recalls the Victorian period in full bloom. Whether a formal drawing room of the late 1860s to 1880s with matching period pieces, or the more eclectic parlor of the 1890s with its mix-and-match approach, High Style leaves no doubt that every element of your decor is firmly rooted in the nineteenth century.

Formal High Style calls to mind plushly upholstered furniture with dark wood trim, opulent window dressings, and traditional, tasteful accessories. The High Style parlor with romantic overtones and the parlor displaying exotic influences are products of the reform movements that ushered in change in Victorian decorating during the late nine-

Above: Today's living room can be infused with Victorian spirit through texture and color. Here, wicker chairs, table, and a small trunk introduce late-nineteenth-century materials in an updated version that blends nicely with the striped sofa and accent pieces.

Opposite: An intimate corner is embellished with the best of Victorian design—art-glass windows, an eye-catching carpet that complements the beautiful wallpaper, and a harmonious blend of furnishings and accessories.

teenth century. A romantic High Style parlor, like the more formal room, makes full use of the background—walls, floors, and windows—to set the tone.

More than simply an indication of wealth, these late Victorian parlors embraced the adventurous, the aesthetic, the intellectual, the hopelessly romantic, and the sophisticated all at the same time.

In contrast to creating an entire room in Victorian period style, introducing Victorian details into an otherwise modern, eclectic, or country setting allows you to have the best of both worlds.

"Modern," referring here to contemporary furnishings and interiors, has moved away from the minimal approach that was popularized during previous decades. With the 1990s tendency to enjoy nesting and to lavish greater attention on our homes, a minimal decorating scheme often falls short in conveying warmth and comfort.

The eclectic parlor or living room actually takes its cue from the late nineteenth century, when Victorians first reveled in mixing styles. Eclectic style affords you the opportunity to blend furnishings from different periods, keeping size, wood tones, and fabric colors in mind. A harmonious blend, not glaring differences, is the goal.

The many facets of modern-day country decorating allow for a creative blend of Victorian embellishments. While "country" signified primitive furnishings and accessories just a few decades ago, this style has since matured. Country decorating now displays European influence, rustic charm, or traditional restraint. In addition, country Victorian has emerged as a style all its own and is usually associated with masses of cozy wicker furnishings; sisal or rag area rugs; crazy quilts; plush, comfortable chairs upholstered in flowered chintz; and wallpapers with delicate floral mini prints or stripes. This style is a combination of sturdy, functional pieces and easy-care fabrics.

The careful attention to detail and lavish decorations that have come to be associated with the proper Victorian parlor was a well-orchestrated blend of several elements designed to complement one another. Historical aspects such as wall treatments, flooring, ceilings, lighting, window dressing, furnishings, and decorative accessories were crucial in achieving just the right look.

As we view each of these elements more closely, a "then and now" approach offers information and suggestions to achieve smashing results—whether your goal is a High Style parlor or a few carefully chosen items that convey the spirit of the Victorian age.

"When a room is properly papered,

curtained, and carpeted, it

may be said to be three-quarters

furnished."

Marion Harland
The Cottage Kitchen, *1883*

While this living room may be anchored by a contemporary sofa, the striped wallpaper treatment combined with a romantic window dressing and a floral carpet produce a decidedly Victorian effect. Carefully chosen accessories such as the decorative screen in the corner complete the setting.

WALL TREATMENTS

Throughout the Victorian period and especially from the 1860s on, wall treatment was the most important aspect in decorating the parlor. Walls were painted or papered—and sometimes both. A wooden wainscot, a paneling used to cover the lower area of a wall, was in vogue from the 1890s through the turn of the century.

The bright colors associated with the candlelit sitting room of the mid-century gave way to lighter shades with the introduction of gaslights; deep, warm tones such as russet, gold, and pumpkin accompanied the reform movements or nature-inspired decorating styles. By the end of the nineteenth century, pale or pastel shades were back in vogue as were the muted greens, earthtones, and gray-blues inspired by the Arts and Crafts Movement.

Prior to 1870, paint color was created by hand using natural pigments, and color choice was somewhat limited. Later in the century, with the introduction of ready-made paints, color possibilities increased dramatically, and suddenly interior walls were on everyone's mind. In 1881 household design expert Clarence Cook wrote *What Shall We Do With Our Walls?* which proved to be a most popular book, and the leading women's magazines frequently published articles devoted to the same subject. The do's and don'ts of choosing color for the parlor followed then-current fashion and were ultimately determined by the level of lighting in the parlor and how much use the room received. If the parlor served as the family sitting room as well as a room in which to entertain, that was to be taken into consideration. The family that was in and out of the parlor all day long would surely benefit from the use of bright, cheerful colors.

Whether painted, papered, treated with a wooden wainscot, or some combination of the above, the parlor walls set the tone for the entire room.

As a romantic look took hold in the parlor during the 1870s and 1880s, wallpaper patterns and colors, as well as paint colors, changed considerably. Ready-made paints could be purchased in deep, sensuous shades such as russet, peacock blue, plum, olive, and terra-cotta. The romantic parlor was a blend of a dominant color and one or more less

"Intricate forms should be accompanied by quiet color, and variety of hue should be chastened by the plainest possible outlines. In color, wall-papers should relieve without violently opposing that of the furniture and hangings by which they are surrounded. There should be one dominant hue in the room, to which all others introduced are subordinate."

Charles L. Eastlake
Hints on Household Taste,
Fourth (Revised) Edition, 1878

This formal setting is enhanced by the addition of a floral wallcovering and a molded chair rail. Deeper shades of color are found in the rug, and the ceiling molding and door frames have been painted to complement the wallpaper.

intense colors, which made full use of this new palette. The tripartite or three-part horizontal wall treatment, featuring dado, field, and frieze, became the preferred way of displaying color and pattern.

In decorating today's formal High Style parlor, consider authentic color combinations that reflect a French-inspired Rococo or Renaissance period room where two colors

Opposite: A simple yet genteel wall treatment of white paint with a frieze at the ceiling creates a lovely background for the formal appointments of this drawing room. The colors found in the frieze are echoed in the window dressings, floral carpet, and furnishings. The result is pure High Style Victorian.

Right: This eclectic setting is enriched by a typical Victorian wall treatment, which combines wooden wainscoting with wide-striped wallpaper. This traditional design element adds just a hint of Victorian gentility to the room, making it suitable for entertaining as well as good old-fashioned relaxation.

were used in harmony or contrast. Colors found next to each other on the color wheel, such as yellow and gold, or colors opposite each other, like crimson and green or violet and yellow, reflect the spirit of a more traditional, formal room. Yellow can be especially attractive with dark wood furnishings.

Wallpaper for the formal High Style parlor might include a striped pattern, a woodgrain design, a boldly colorful floral pattern reminiscent of Rococo Revival style, or an abstract nature theme. Wallpapers used in a formal setting generally feature light shades such as pale blue, gray, light green, or yellow.

In creating a High Style romantic parlor, follow the Victorian lead and dress your walls in three distinct horizontal sections. Several mail-order wallpaper companies spe-

cialize in Victorian patterns that can be used to create a dado, fill, and frieze, or you can opt for a wooden wainscoting, painted fill, and paper frieze. A chair rail (a decorative, molded wooden strip used around the perimeter of the room to protect the wall from being marked by the back of a chair), with walls papered or painted above and below, will achieve the same effect. Keep in mind the warm shades that predominated during the era of the tripartite wall.

The wallpapers most appropriate in the tripartite treatment include flat, small-scale designs, such as geometric patterns; abstract designs featuring flowers, birds, or foliage; and Japanesque patterns with Oriental fans, vases, or nature themes. Authentic

nineteenth-century patterns are being reproduced today, or you may choose a contemporary pattern that follows the same design principles.

Another popular alternative is the use of embossed papers, known as Lincrusta and Anaglypta, as a dado. In imitation of High Style plasterwork, Frederick Walton created Lincrusta, a linseed oil paper that was backed with canvas, in 1877. Ten years later the lighter-weight Anaglypta was developed using a backing of paper fibers. Victorian household experts compared the appearance of these papers to stamped leather and praised their elegant beauty as well as their durability and strength. Lincrusta and Anaglypta are both being manufactured today, and

while Lincrusta was routinely used in Victorian entryways, it's perfectly suitable for the parlor and can be a stunning alternative to a wainscot. Once applied, Lincrusta can be painted with an oil-based paint in the color of your choice. The lighter Anaglypta paper is ideal as a frieze and should be painted with latex paint. Both are available in a variety of nineteenth-century patterns.

To evoke the simpler style in vogue during the 1890s, dress walls with a wainscot or frieze, but not both, and rely on light or pastel shades such as gray, lilac, light blue, light green, silver, fawn, rose, or pale olive. The abstract wallpaper patterns popular during the 1870s and 1880s continued to be used during the last decade of the century, albeit in simplified form. In addition, solid-color canvas papers became popular and are ideal in creating a turn-of-the-century Arts and Crafts parlor.

Along with the mail-order companies that specialize in Victorian-style wallpapers, many noteworthy design firms and respected manufacturers make their products available through retail stores and decorating centers.

Wallpapers commonly used in creating Victorian style include machine-printed papers, which are manufactured for consistent pattern-matching with colors that will not vary from roll to roll, and hand-printed papers, which are authentic recreations of nineteenth-century papers using the same process that the Victorians used. Hand-printed wallpapers are not as sturdy as machine-printed papers and should be used in areas that don't receive a lot of wear and tear. Wallpaper borders are also ideal for creating a chair-rail effect on a painted wall.

Since choosing wallpaper can be difficult, concentrate on studios or pattern books devoted to Victorian patterns and themes.

"Wilton carpet: A kind of carpet made in England, and so called from the place which is the chief seat of their manufacture. They are woolen velvets with variegated colors."

Catharine E. Beecher & Harriet Beecher Stowe
American Woman's Home, *1869*

Evoking the late Victorian era, a hardwood floor is dressed with a sumptuous Oriental rug. The romantic High Style is carried further with period furnishings, antique accessories, and a shuttered window treatment that complements the room's handsome wood tones.

FLOORING

As the Industrial Revolution gained speed during the mid-nineteenth century, decorating options for middle-class Victorians increased considerably.

Early on, parlor floors were painted or covered with floorcloths, carpet matting (which was created from woven plant fibers), druggets (made of coarse wool cloth or wool and flax), or ingrain carpets (flat, woven carpets made in narrow strips sewn together). In the homes of the well-to-do, floors were covered with pile carpets commonly called Wiltons or Brussels.

As wall-to-wall carpeting became more affordable, it was considered a necessity in the proper parlor. Large floral-patterned carpets in various shades of a single color, as well as multicolored examples, were popular during the 1860s and 1870s. Experts suggested that dark colors would complement furnishings particularly well.

During the last quarter of the nineteenth century, carpeting was suddenly considered old-fashioned, as hardwood floors with Oriental area rugs became the darling of a new era in interior design. That's not to say everyone rushed to remove their carpeting, for underneath were softwood floors that remained to be dealt with. Creative measures were suggested, including dressing carpets with an attractive border or simulating a hardwood look with paints or narrow strips of wood strategically placed around the perimeter of the room. New homes constructed during the 1880s and 1890s occasionally featured parquet floors or a wood-strip carpeting in a parquet pattern placed atop a less-expensive floor.

In decorating today's Victorian-style parlor, especially when a formal look is desired, using wall-to-wall carpeting with large

beauty. Available in a wide array of colors and patterns, your choice in rugs is almost limitless. Remember to select your rug to mix harmoniously with furnishings, rather than to dominate the room.

Take Victorian style one step further and consider seasonal decorating. You can remove your Oriental rug during the warmer months and replace it with sisal matting just as the Victorians would have done.

If your home has wall-to-wall carpeting, layering for a rich, romantic look is a

geometric, floral, or foliage designs can add a plush, elegant look. Victorian-inspired patterns are readily available in a variety of colors and designs. Take care in making your decision, since carpeting is something we live with for a long time. Let your own good taste and personal preferences be your guide.

For a High Style parlor with a romantic look, a rug of Japanese or Chinese design can be the ideal choice. Modern reproductions offer excellent quality and unsurpassed

A small area rug clearly defines this cozy corner for two. The simplicity of the creamy rug works beautifully with upholstered easy chairs, and the fabric is repeated in the window dressing. Victorian style is at the very heart of this intimate grouping.

"A carpet should always be chosen as background, upon which the other articles of furniture are to be placed—it should vie with nothing, but rather give value to all objects coming in contact with it. Composed of somber shades, and tones, and treated essentially as a flat surface, it exerts a most valuable, though subordinate influence upon all the other decorations of the day."

Godey's Lady's Book, *August 1855*

wonderful idea. Place an Oriental rug or several smaller area rugs about the room to define conversation areas, cover traffic paths, or dress a cozy corner.

In a modern, eclectic, or country decorating scheme, an Oriental rug is an elegant way of drawing the past into the present day.

Since styles overlapped throughout the nineteenth century, there is no wrong way of dressing your floors. Personal choice is paramount, taking into consideration the needs of your household, whether or not you own your home, and so on. Keep in mind that quality and longevity are synonymous when it comes to carpeting and rugs; it's worth investing in finely made coverings for your floor. When purchasing an Oriental rug, look for one made of wool. It will be soft to the touch (rather than stiff), dirt and stain resistant, and will last for many years.

CEILINGS

Today we tend to give our ceilings a coat of white paint and then forget about them—until it's time to paint again. Not so with the Victorians, who considered the ceiling yet another surface to be adorned when decorating the parlor.

＊

A beautiful needlepoint rug takes center stage in this classic country setting, adding the same graceful charm found in parlors more than a century ago. The large floral motif was popular in the early Victorian era and serves as an elegant background for furnishings of varied styles.

With ceilings often twelve to fourteen feet high during the early Victorian period, household experts found a white ceiling acceptable, but considered painting it a lighter shade of the color on the parlor walls an even better solution. In addition, wood, papier-mâché, or plasterwork medallions, usually two feet (0.6m) in diameter, were featured in the center of the ceiling, often serving as a decorative backdrop to an ornate chandelier. Medallions were typically carved or molded in a plain or floral design, and a wooden or plasterwork cornice was suggested to separate the walls and the ceiling visually. The cornice was usually painted a darker shade than the wall to highlight the division of space, or painted gold for a richer look.

The practice of decorating ceilings continued throughout the nineteenth century, and by the 1870s and 1880s experts still favored painting the ceiling in lighter shades of the wall color; lavender, peach, gray, and blue were then popular colors.

Other decorative practices came into vogue, such as "striping," which involved painting thin strips of color around the edge of the cornice to further accentuate the separation between wall and ceiling. Center medallions continued to be popular, and machine-made examples as well as factory-produced cornices were readily available and easy to install.

The use of wallpaper on the ceiling was introduced during the late 1800s, and Victorians were advised to be cautious in selecting such a paper, since harmony was the objective rather than a bold, shocking change. This practice of employing wallpaper on the ceiling continued throughout the 1890s with a shift towards simplicity. Center medallions were now considered passé and the elaborately papered ceiling garish.

Above: The high ceiling in this Victorian Revival parlor is graced with a striking center medallion, gilded for a formal effect. The cornice has been painted and "striped" to clearly define the separation of space between walls and ceiling.

Right: This eclectic parlor combines traditional nineteenth-century touches with a hint of exotica. Ceiling and walls are papered to give the room a unified appearance and play host to an array of worldly treasures, including a lacquered table, a stuffed peacock, and an ornate guitar. The overall effect is quite romantic and very much Victorian.

Instead, a return to the painted ceiling was called for, in a light tint that would harmonize with the wallpaper. Others recommended papering the ceiling and carrying the subdued pattern down the wall to a picture rail, a decorative wood strip from which artwork could be hung.

When considering the ceiling in a formal High Style parlor, a modern reproduction medallion can be a perfect accent. These are available in a variety of nineteenth-century motifs, are simple to install, and, by virtue of their light weight, are easy to work with. Your center medallion can be painted to match the ceiling, appear in an accent color, or be enhanced with gilding for a sumptuous, upscale look.

The romantic parlor is the ideal setting for a papered ceiling or a ceiling painted as the Victorians would have done—in a light color to harmonize with the walls or wallpaper. Adding a decorative cornice or molding around the room will heighten the effect; if you prefer a scaled-down look, choose a wallpaper pattern that can be carried down the wall (how far down is determined by the height of your ceiling) to a picture rail. A ceiling paper with a center design in an octagonal, round, or rectangular shape (reminiscent of a metal or plaster medallion) with a corresponding pattern radiating outward from the center can be eye-catching, as can a more subtle pattern that adds charm but less drama.

In adapting nineteenth-century ceiling treatments for today's homes, restraint is the key word. A medallion and cornice can be a positive addition to an otherwise modern setting, but a ceiling paper may be too heavy-handed. If a subtle pattern is used, ceiling

paper may be well suited to a contemporary country parlor, where this unusual touch lends a quiet Victorian presence.

Left: A plain, round center medallion possesses an understated beauty that gives a finished look to this tasteful drawing room. The simple concentric circles serve as a wonderful backdrop for the ornate hanging fixture— undoubtedly a converted gasolier.

Below: This formal parlor showcases numerous Victorian touches, including a combination of lighting—from beautiful wall sconces for candles to electric lamps on parlor tables. The romantic glow of candlelight is often preferable in intimate settings.

LIGHTING

Lighting in the nineteenth-century home evolved from candlelight in the early 1800s to kerosene lamps by the 1850s, and on to gasoliers (hanging gas lamps) in the later part of the century. Electricity was common in urban homes by the late 1890s but remained unavailable in most rural areas until the 1920s and 1930s.

The Victorians devised a combination of ways to light their homes. Candlelight was fashionable for decades, and was often used with oil or gas fixtures to enhance the lighting in the parlor and cast a warm glow.

Kerosene lamps in a variety of styles were thought to be a household necessity, and the parlor was usually host to stand or table lamps, bracket lamps, or a brass chandelier. As styles changed, so did the fashion regarding lamps. Shades were produced in a wide range of decorative glass, including translucent, opaque, opalescent, and alabaster, and bases or pedestals were typically glass or metal. Ornamental embellishments such as figural stems or cut-glass prisms were used on kerosene lamps placed in the dining room and parlor. What we commonly refer to as "Gone With the Wind" lamps were popular during the 1880s and 1890s, and were often found in the parlor as well. These kerosene lamps had painted glass bodies and globes with decorative features. They got their name because one appeared in the movie *Gone With the Wind* (though it was something of an anachronism, since these lamps did not come into use until well after the Civil War).

Gasolier hanging fixtures were common in the late-nineteenth-century parlor or sitting room, and even though urban residences were lit by gas, often an assortment of kerosene lamps was used to achieve the necessary lighting. By this time lamps were being decorated with fabric shades trimmed with fringe or lace. Gasoliers were quite fancy, and often included prisms, small figurals, or decorative glass globes.

Once electric power became available, Art Nouveau–inspired lamps became popular. These artistic, often flamboyant table lamps sported art-glass shades or shades with reverse paintings, and while the middle class could hardly afford a stunning example produced by Louis C. Tiffany, other studios and manufacturers began turning out adaptations based on the art-glass concept.

In today's formal High Style parlor, vintage or reproduction lamps and fixtures provide adequate lighting as well as the right tone. If you have your heart set on an authentic piece, check with antiques dealers who specialize in this area, or visit an architectural salvage emporium. Restoration experts can repair damaged fixtures as well as

Above: This appealing window dressing uses layers of fabrics for a romantic effect. A lace undercurtain, held in check by a decorative brass pin, is allowed to puddle at the floor. The rod-pocket outer curtain, hinting at the colors in the carpet and furnishings, is likewise pulled aside.

Opposite: Embellished with glass prisms and silver-toned candles, this exquisite brass chandelier is the most ornate piece in the room. The parlor is further accessorized with candlesticks and a kerosene lamp.

convert them for electrical use. A chandelier hung from the center of the room (at least seven feet [2.1m] from the floor), and table lamps (such as the Gone With the Wind style) carefully placed about the room are both elegant and lovely.

The romantic parlor reminiscent of the 1890s is the ideal setting for an art-glass lamp or two. While noted antique examples are rare, modern reproductions displaying the work of skilled artisans are available. Considered much more than a decorative accessory, these handcrafted reproductions are an investment that will undoubtedly increase in value over time.

An outstanding lighting fixture can draw attention in any room. To recall the spirit of Victorian times in a modern, eclectic, or country-style parlor, consider displaying a collection of kerosene lamps (common glass examples are still plentiful), or placing an art-glass table lamp in a spot where it is sure to be admired.

Keep in mind the spirit of the Victorian parlor—cozy, comfortable, and romantic, possibly with several conversation areas. Background lighting with a variety of wall, ceiling, or table lamps (in differing degrees of intensity) will create ambience. In addition, accent lighting that spotlights a collection, a piece of art, or a pleasant corner of the room is an ideal way to draw attention to a special Victorian touch.

WINDOW TREATMENTS

How the Victorians loved to dress their windows! The art of window dressing during much of the nineteenth century can be described in one word—excessive. Granted, the middle class could rarely afford the opulent masses of curtains and decorative

"It will be a very pretty thing, now,

to cut out of the same material as

your lounge, sets of lambrequins...a

kind of pendent curtain-top...

to put over the windows, which are to

be embellished with white muslin

curtains. The cornices to your

windows can be simple strips of wood

covered with paper to match

the bordering of your room, and the

lambrequins, made of chintz like

the lounge, can be trimmed with

fringe....A tassel at the lowest point

improves the appearance....The in-

fluence of white-muslin curtains in

giving an air of grace and elegance

to a room is astonishing."

Catharine E. Beecher &
Harriet Beecher Stowe
The American Woman's Home,
1869

embellishments that appeared in popular magazines, but many households tried to imitate current fashions to some degree.

During the early Victorian period, curtains (slightly longer than floor length) were used with a wooden cornice and a fabric valance. Decorative brass pins were employed to pull or loop the curtains back. As the century progressed, an increasingly rich look evolved from the popular taste for Rococo Revival and Renaissance Revival interiors. Layers were added to window dressing as a decorative feature and in a practical attempt to block drafts and protect furnishings from sunlight. By mid-century both shades and undercurtains (also called "glass curtains") of lace or muslin were used in conjunction with the more formal, floor-length curtain and the valance, now known as a "lambrequin," which was embellished with trimmings or tassels.

With the Eastlake Movement came the call to simplify. Ornate lambrequins were considered vulgar and tasteless, and ornamentation in the form of trims and tassels fell out of favor. Charles Eastlake recommended a return to simple floor-length curtains attached to a small rod with rings, which could easily be left open or pulled shut.

The height of opulence, this spacious Victorian Revival–style parlor makes full use of a layered window treatment for an elegant High Style effect. A lace undercurtain is topped with rich fabric curtains sporting a fringed lambrequin. This arrangement is strikingly highlighted with a lush red swag that repeats the color in the sofa.

Opposite: Lace panels and a dressy, fringed fabric swag recall late-nineteenth-century style in this well-appointed parlor. The panels are gathered with delicate pins and gold fabric cord, and are allowed to cascade to the floor. Note, too, that the swag is a deeper shade of the fabric used on the gentleman's Rococo Revival armchair and the dainty sidechair at the piano.

Right: By the late Victorian era the popular sentiment "less is more" found interior design moving toward simplicity. Lace panels proved the ideal window dressing, combining the Victorian love of pattern and texture with the light touch recommended in decorating.

During the last decade of the century lace was especially popular, and lace panels were frequently hung inside the window frame, reaching down only as far as the windowsill. Venetian curtains, what we call balloon curtains today, were also popular during the 1890s. Overall, window dressings of the late Victorian era were less fussy compared with earlier decades. The typical middle-class parlor made use of a lace undercurtain, a less-formal outer curtain, and a pleated or pinch-pleat valance or swag.

Window shutters, blinds, and shades were used throughout the Victorian period, depending upon the mistress' inclination. These window treatments are particularly useful for controlling the amount of light a window admits.

Portieres were in vogue during the 1890s, and these curtains in doorways were used to block drafts as well as to enhance the appearance of the room. A portiere suspended from rings on a rod may have appeared at the entrance to the parlor or between a front parlor and rear sitting room. While fabric examples may well have been functional as well as decorative, rope cord portieres were clearly an accessory.

In creating Victorian style in today's parlor, a formal look will be enhanced by using an undercurtain, such as lace panels, floor-length drapes, and a fabric or wood valance. A valance with elegant drapes, looped back during the day to expose a pleasing view (minus the undercurtain), is another alternative. Ultimately, your choice should be determined by how elaborate a window treatment you desire—and are willing to maintain. The Victorian period ushered in so very many styles and possibilities that even an authentic period room has the luxury of options when it comes to window dressing.

The romantic High Style parlor is the perfect setting for lace—and lots of it. Lace curtains with a lace or fabric swag or festoon are stunning. A lace undercurtain with drapes is also in keeping with a romantic theme, as is a balloon shade or even bamboo shades, which evoke a hint of the exotic.

Considerations to keep in mind, regardless of the effect you're trying to achieve, are whether you need a window treatment to guard against drafts, a purely decorative treatment, one to show off or hide a view, and the amount of time you plan to devote to upkeep.

Lace is especially effective in conveying the romance of the Victorian era, and lace panels can be the perfect touch in a non-Victorian setting.

FURNISHINGS

The very best furniture in the Victorian home was reserved for the parlor. The various styles that came and went throughout the nineteenth century were on display in proper parlors all across the country as a tribute to good taste and as an obvious show of wealth. As each new style was introduced, Victorians of considerable means invested in the latest fashion and often relegated older pieces to other rooms in the house or used them in furnishing summer homes. Most families, however, would have gone broke in an attempt to keep pace with ever-changing trends, and opted instead to blend a new piece of furniture here and there to evoke the spirit of the latest style. As a result, a parlor furnished in Rococo Revival style might have included a Renaissance-inspired chair or two, and the parlor given over to Renaissance Revival style may have been embellished with a Japanesque wicker chair.

Although this mix-and-match approach in regard to furnishings was quite common, today's parlor outfitted in a formal revival style is enhanced by allowing the beauty of the style to take center stage. To dress this setting with a hodgepodge of furnishings

———※———

Undoubtedly the most impressive room in the house, this parlor is outfitted with gilded wood Rococo Revival settee and chairs. Embellished with carved floral crests and curved legs, and upholstered in a rich damask, these furnishings were in vogue during the mid-century period and were especially popular in the South.

from later periods would detract from the air of elegance and opulence. With this in mind, look for a Rococo Revival sofa or settee with a serpentine (gently curved) or medallion back and gracefully curved legs. Delicate walnut, rosewood, or mahogany side chairs complete the "set." The side chairs typically had upholstered, oval-shaped backs surrounded by wood with a carved floral crest. Noteworthy, too, is the fact that many such pieces were upholstered with horsehair (actually a combination of horsehair and fabric), which was long-wearing, shiny in appearance, and actually quite slippery to sit on. Rococo Revival, then, is best identified by its numerous floral and foliage carvings and its gentle, curving lines.

Renaissance Revival–style furnishings are more substantial, characterized by ex-

look. Simplified Eastlake-style furniture manufactured in oak, cherry, or walnut and embellished with machine-carved incised lines is perfectly at home with furnishings and accessories that salute the exotic, the aesthetic, or Art Nouveau. Subdued wicker and handsome golden oak blend beautifully in the eclectic parlor, providing a bridge between light and airy styles and strong, bold looks. The straightforward lines of Arts and Crafts furniture, on the other hand, can be best appreciated when standing alone.

There are numerous ways to acquire furniture for the proper Victorian parlor. Refer

Above: Victorian ambience combines with neo-classical armchairs to produce striking results in this intimate seating area near the warmth of the fire.

Right: Adorned with fringe and tassels, these matching one-armed chairs are splendid with their tufted, velvet upholstery. The rich red color is repeated in the opulent window dressings, accenting the room's High Style flair.

treme ornamentation and straight legs. Settees with wooden-framed upholstered backs crowned with a molded crest or pediment are a hallmark of this period. Elegant fabrics were featured on these square-backed walnut pieces rather than horsehair, which had fallen out of favor.

If your taste falls within the realm of the reform movements, your parlor can have a less formal, but more romantic, even eclectic

to the source directory in the back of the book for information on where to purchase both antique and reproduction pieces. In addition, auctions and antiques shows or shops offer many possibilities for uncovering vintage furniture. Inspect each piece carefully to determine condition and authenticity.

Many noted manufacturers have been introducing lines of furniture with the Victorian parlor in mind. The advent of Victorian Revival style has prompted the display of showroom furniture with romantic appeal and richly elegant design.

After choosing the style of furniture for your parlor and deciding if you'll invest in antiques or reproductions, fabric is likely to be your next consideration. With your color scheme in mind, the more formal, revival-style furnishings (Gothic, Rococo, and Renaissance) are best dressed when upholstered in a rich, raised-pattern brocade displaying an elegant floral motif; a cotton, or silk damask (a soft, flat-patterned fabric, which is stunning in a delicate shade); sateen (a sturdier version of satin); a tapestry fabric with a multicolored pictorial scene or pattern design; or a plush velvet in a warm, luxurious tone. Furniture is often the most dramatic touch in a formal High Style setting, and a sumptuous upholstery is called for.

In the romantic parlor, furniture upholstered in deep tones or in pale shades that exhibit the small nature-inspired designs reminiscent of the reform movements can be the perfect complement to warm, painted walls or an exquisite wallpaper. Subtle Oriental patterns are also lovely, and a patterned chintz or damask is the fabric of choice for upholstery.

For parlors or living rooms with a modern or eclectic theme, one striking piece of nineteenth-century furniture can be all that's needed to pay tribute to the past. The country style permits a bit more diversity as it mingles beautifully with Victoriana, and wicker, factory-made oak, or an eye-catching piece of Adirondack furniture would be an ideal way to blend nineteenth-century beauty with country simplicity and charm.

DECORATIVE ACCESSORIES AND COLLECTIBLES

The parlor walls were tastefully painted or papered, windows properly dressed, rugs or carpet carefully laid, and furniture and lamps situated just so. Last but far from least, sundry items were called for to accessorize the proper Victorian parlor. Plush fringed or needlework pillows were piled high on sofas and settees; a gilt mirror was placed above the mantel; artwork in the form of oil paintings, lithographs, and needlework was everywhere apparent; and potted palms and ferns decorated cozy corners, displaying a love of nature. Birdcages, books, fresh flowers, colorful throws, pottery, glassware, souvenirs, and handcrafted items embellished the setting to the point of overflow, and created the air of intimacy and romance we find so appealing today.

Victorian women were avid gardeners and excelled at handiwork. Tending indoor plants and creating terrariums was considered educational for children and added poetic beauty to the parlor, library, or sitting room. Nature expeditions were conducted to collect shells, twigs, or moss, which were used in decorating small picture frames for cherished photos.

Needlecraft, whether done to create fancy pillows or the crocheted antimacassars designed to protect delicate upholstery, was an accomplishment Victorian women embraced for practical purposes as well as for good social standing. Not only could they embellish their homes with the fruits of their talent and skill, but their labors proved them industrious and moral.

In today's parlor, decorative accessories are every bit as important in creating Victorian style as they were during the 1800s. Wild abundance or quiet restraint—the choice is yours. Pillows are a must, and needlepoint, tapestry, or fringed examples convey the spirit of the era. Display family photos in vintage or handcrafted frames made with shells, twigs, or mosaics for a personal touch and a hint of the outdoors. Foliage and fresh flowers enhance the

Infused with Victorian spirit, this living room is made more personal and decorative with special books and fresh flowers arranged artfully on tabletops. The nineteenth-century birdcage, a wonderful and whimsical antique, becomes an instant focal point in the room.

Victorian setting, and carefully chosen art-work gracing painted or papered walls can cultivate a formal tone with portraits and nature scenes that suggest artistic bravado; or create an eclectic look with a medley of prints and handcrafted items.

Regarding other decorative accessories, the nineteenth century brought with it a whirlwind of changes and developments. The Industrial Revolution ushered in mass production, and special exhibits opened the world to new cultures. Travel, both abroad and across the country, became possible, and

Absolute comfort abounds in this cozy seating area near the fire. Select oil paintings add a hint of Victorian formality, while decorative and fringed pillows atop the sofa contribute an inviting and fanciful touch. Favorite col-lectibles are close at hand, and the entire scene speaks of solid comfort.

as the income of the typical middle-class fam-ily increased, Victorians were captivated by the overwhelming variety of items that sud-denly became available to them.

The Victorians adored "things." Enthu-siastic collectors, they were charmed by the latest inventions as well as by novelty items imported from other lands. They amassed new belongings with a passion and displayed them or put them to use throughout the house. Fast-forward to the present day and these are the treasured objects we call an-tiques and collectibles.

In the parlor, these cherished mementos from the nineteenth century add yet another dimension to vintage Victorian style. It is a rare Victorian Revivalist indeed who does not covet these enchanting collectibles and look to their charm to personalize the home. Simply put, we surround ourselves with the things we love, just as the Victorians did. We are, after all, kindred spirits.

The proper Victorian parlor was home to a wide assortment of articles depending upon then-current fashion and a lady's own good taste. Today we have the pleasure of building collections that convey the best of Victoriana. Let your pleasure be your guide.

During the nineteenth century, collections of similar items were displayed in the parlor atop mantels and tables, arranged in vignettes, or clustered together on wall-hung shelves and in étagères or simpler whatnots.

Among the more popular items the Victorians delighted in displaying were decorative glass; pottery; photographs; albums full of photos, calling cards, or trade cards; souvenirs; and other ornamental bric-a-brac.

Decorative glass refers to the variety of pressed glass, patterned glass, and colored glassware introduced during the nineteenth century. A favorite among those who strove for good taste, Bohemian glass was imported in large quantities during the late nineteenth century. Bohemian glassworks turned out a variety of crystal and colored glass objects in shades of amber, red, cobalt, and ameythst, which Victorians found especially appealing. In addition, many examples were adorned with engraved patterns such as florals, "deer with trees," "animal and birds with trees," and so on. Captivated by the sultry colors and the delicate designs, Victorians couldn't resist displaying Bohemian glass in a place of honor on the mantel or a prominent tabletop.

Nooks and crannies often provide the perfect place for displaying cherished mementos. Here, a tabletop vignette of beautifully framed photos not only personalizes living space but recalls the Victorian penchant for grouping favorite objects.

Majolica pottery was being produced in Great Britain by the 1850s, but it wasn't until the 1876 Centennial Exposition in Philadelphia that a record number of Victorians got their first glimpse of these beautiful wares. Colorful and nature-inspired, with high-relief decorations and a clear lead glaze, majolica was imported from England and France, and was eventually produced by a number of American firms as well. This unusual pottery was extremely popular from the late 1870s through 1900.

Common examples included pitchers, platters, plates, leaf-shaped plates, teapots, cups and saucers, bowls, compotes, planters, vases, candlesticks, calling card holders, and jardinieres. Often used for display rather than as intended (majolica was too beautiful to cover up), plates were lined on a shelf, pitchers held bouquets of fresh flowers, and planters and jardinieres proved ideal for the lush foliage that brought the freshness of the outdoors into the Victorian parlor. Embellished with everything from flowers, leaves, and fruit to shells, seaweed, birds, and fish, majolica appealed to the Victorians' aesthetic sensibilities and proved worthy of a place of honor in the proper Victorian parlor.

Nineteenth-century photographs offer us the best possible glimpse of the past. Victorian ladies and gentlemen, dressed in their finest garb with just a hint of a smile or a gleam in their eye, pose ever so formally for the photographer. These cherished possessions were a novel way of capturing a loved one for eternity, and this appealed greatly to the Victorians' sense of family. Family photos were proudly displayed throughout the parlor and were a comfort as well as objects to be admired.

Some of the techniques and materials used in early photography resulted in photos of archival quality. Such processes included carbon prints (1860s on), with sepia, purple-brown, or black tones, and platinum prints (late 1800s) with soft gray tones. These photos can generally be found in good condition, but photos produced by earlier methods have sadly faded.

Victorian photographs are charming in and of themselves and can lend a sense of history to any room. Victorians displayed them prominently on the mantel or clustered on a special tabletop.

If the conversation in the parlor seemed to lag or the hostess wished to change the subject, the family photo album or a scrap album full of select calling cards or advertising trade cards could be passed around the room. Callers could admire these keepsakes and a lively conversation might ensue. Albums of the late nineteenth century were decorative, with celluloid covers or leather covers embossed with gold. The colorful cards sported vibrant tones thanks to a new printing process called chromolithography. The Victorians adored color, and these cards were collected because of their novelty and the endearing images often depicted.

The photo album or scrap album was typically placed atop a table draped with a lace scarf or shawl, or perhaps casually set on a chair, ever ready to be passed about the room or to receive a new treasure.

As the Victorians began to travel, taking in new sights and visiting expositions, returning home with souvenirs was proof that they had the wherewithal to venture away from home. Everything from souvenir spoons and fans to commemorative plates and bric-a-brac were transported back to the Victorian parlor, where they were displayed amid the carefully arranged clutter.

Other collectibles were also on display in the parlor. Items such as candlesticks were often grouped atop the mantel. Made of silver, glass, brass, or pottery, candlesticks never went out of fashion, and were often passed from one generation to the next.

With the clamor to exhibit an appreciation of other cultures and the arts, exotica in the form of small carved animals were in vogue during the late 1800s. Made of ivory or wood, these novelty items exuded good taste, and given their size, "the more the merrier" was the consensus.

Perhaps collected during travels, trinkets and souvenirs with an Oriental feel combine with nineteenth-century furnishings to create a comfortable and eye-catching corner where exotica is the theme.

Collecting is highly personal and a matter close to the heart. These are but a few suggestions intended to provide food for thought in personalizing your own Victorian parlor. Regardless of where your passion lies, study your area of interest well, buy the very best you can afford, and seek out dealers who specialize in Victoriana. Above all, enjoy—just as the Victorians did.

The Dining Room

Handsome, formal, and elegant—this was the Victorian dining room.

As a hive of social activity, the dining room was the other room in the house, second only to the parlor, where attention to detail was paramount. Dinner parties and afternoon teas and receptions were the most popular manner of entertaining in an era that found home the setting for numerous genial gatherings. Elaborate tableware and formal dinners comprising several courses required the perfect backdrop. The dining room was a model of genteel taste in decoration, substantial furnishings, and carefully chosen accessories. Deportment in the dining room referred not only to one's behavior but to the manner in which this all-important room was dressed.

The pleasure of your company is requested…enter the Victorian dining room and enjoy a glimpse of the past. Savor the promise of dining in this special place and note the Victorian passion for detail.

The epitome of the Victorian dining room, this setting includes a well-appointed table, handsome furnishings, a tasteful window dressing, and a thoroughly polished backdrop. Impressive details, from the floral arrangement to the display atop the elaborate sideboard, impart gentility.

The History of the Victorian Dining Room

The eighteenth-century homes of the Colonial era grew from the one-room hall to include a separate "keeping room," or kitchen, and a sitting room for family activity and entertaining. As homes of the well-to-do grew larger, the early nineteenth century brought wider use of a room devoted to dining. Depending upon locale and architectural style, the early-Victorian-period dining room was located on the first floor, close to the kitchen, or as in many urban row houses, the dining room was situated in a half-basement, or "English style" basement. This was also the arrangement in many of the large homes of the wealthy. By the 1870s the formal dining room was usually included on the ground floor, and if the kitchen was still relegated to the basement area, a dumbwaiter was used to transport meals upstairs.

Quite often rectangular in shape, many dining rooms were found in the midsection of the house, often accessible through the parlor or a short walk down the center hall. A door or passageway typically led to the butler's pantry or kitchen.

The Victorian dining room was much more than simply a room in which to entertain guests. The social drama and code of etiquette associated with the Victorian era played itself out most noticeably in this elegant setting.

The host and hostess extended formal, written invitations to dine (and less formal invitations to a tea party), and the guest replied in kind, regardless of whether the invitation was accepted or declined. A timely response was imperative.

"Dinner, being the grand solid meal of the day, is a matter of considerable importance; and a well-served table is a striking index of human ingenuity and resource."

Mrs. Isabella Beeton
Beeton's Book of Household
Management, *1861*

The dinner party usually included six to ten guests; it was considered poor taste to allow the number at the table to swell to thirteen due to the superstition surrounding this number. The primary objective, of course, was to invite only as many guests as could be comfortably seated without crowding.

On the evening of the dinner party, guests were shown to the parlor to await everyone's arrival and the announcement

This inviting dining room has been lavishly prepared for dinner guests. The table rug is in place, the table has been draped with not one but two white cloths, and the finest tableware is on display. Fresh flowers softly scent the room, and at the last moment, perhaps a fire will be lit in the fireplace.

that dinner was served. The host or hostess would escort guests to the dining room, where name cards indicated a carefully planned seating arrangement. Guests were assembled around the table in groupings intended to promote pleasant and entertaining conversation. The success of the party, in fact, was usually determined by whether good conversation flowed freely throughout the course of the evening.

During the early Victorian period the dining room table was laden with dishes. In preparing for the meal, a "table rug" was carefully placed underneath the table and the table itself was covered with two white tablecloths, one atop the other. The castor set or a celery stand was placed on the center of the table and individual place settings were arranged. Salt stands were situated at the four corners of the table while jellies and pickles were placed at diagonal corners. The side table groaned under the weight of the additional tableware that would be needed during the course of the dinner. The host carved meats, and he and the hostess passed dishes to their guests. Servants were on hand to clear and reset the table as needed. When dinner was finished the table was cleared and one of the tablecloths removed; dessert dishes were then set in place. Following dessert, the second tablecloth was removed, and fruit and coffee were placed on the bare tabletop. These rituals and elaborate meals were thought excessive by critics who called for simpler meals with far fewer offerings.

The 1870s witnessed the popularity of dinner *a la Russe*, in which everything was placed on the sideboards and servants did all the carving. In this way the host and hostess could devote full attention to their guests, and a more elaborate centerpiece could grace the table.

A white damask or lace tablecloth and, of course, the best china were used. Flowers, mosses, or ferns were often arranged as a centerpiece, and an epergne (a tiered glass or metal dish for fruit or flowers) was especially fashionable during the late nineteenth century. Elaborate stands of bonbons or other sweets were often set on each side of the table.

Generally, soup was served, followed by fish, then meat or game. Vegetables were served with the meat or as a separate dish, and then a salad was presented. After dinner the tablecloth was brushed to remove crumbs, and dessert was served. Finger bowls were placed at each setting before fruit was set on the table, and finally a rich coffee was poured.

By the end of the nineteenth century, critics were still campaigning for simpler dinner parties and felt that any obvious attempt to display social status was in poor taste. The purpose of dinner was, after all, to promote agreeable conversation among friends, rather than to dazzle acquaintances with an ostentatious show of wealth.

When guests sat down to dine, their surroundings were ideally a comfortable blend of harmonious colors and elegant furniture, tableware, and accessories that intimated at prosperity and good moral standing. The dining room itself, throughout much of the century, was decorated in rich shades such as deep red, dark blue, gold, or various tints of green, which were complemented by dark woodwork or, often, wooden wainscoting. Wallpaper was frequently used in the dining room, and during earlier periods a scenic paper was favored. Later, the reform movements inspired wallpaper with small floral or foliage motifs, and in addition, Lincrusta embossed paper was popular as a dado treatment. By the turn of the century, dark colors

---

"The dinner hour will completely test the refinement, the culture and good breeding which the individual may possess. To appear advantageously at the table, the person must not only understand the laws of etiquette, but he must have the advantage of polite society."

Thos. E. Hill
Hill's Manual of Social and
Business Forms, *1888*

---

in the dining room were thought dreary and the experts called for lighter shades of blue, yellow, or red, which would be "cheerful." With this advice came the practice of using solid colors or a two-toned treatment on dining room walls.

During the second half of the nineteenth century, fine artwork such as the still life seen here atop the mantel were considered de rigueur in the Victorian dining room. Quality was not equated with quantity—a few carefully selected pieces were all that was called for.

Dining room floors were carpeted during the early Victorian years with a dark color featuring large floral designs or geometric patterns. By the 1870s hardwood floors, sometimes in a parquet design, were preferred, and were partially covered by a rug; an Oriental rug was wellsuited to the dining room where the deep colors and patterns contributed to the overall feeling of warmth.

Window treatments were often elaborate, just as they were in the parlor, and the use of rich color was extended to the curtain fabric. The grandeur of this room was enhanced by windows dressed in layer after layer of fabric and lace.

Lighting was usually provided by a chandelier, wall brackets or sconces, candles, or kerosene lamps with shades. Strong lighting was objectionable in the dining room. Subdued lighting, however, contributed to the overall sense of comfort and relaxation, and encouraged intimate conversation.

During the early decades of the Victorian age family portraits were favored as a dignified, decorative touch, but as the nineteenth century progressed, still-life paintings of fruit, nature scenes, game, and fowl became popular. Two or three excellent pieces of art were all that was required. By the dawn of the twentieth century the critics felt strongly that paintings featuring game, wild animals, or fish were out of place in the dining room. They professed that such scenes would detract from enjoyment of the meal.

Furnishing the dining room called for substantial pieces that were both handsome and elegant. The first Victorian dining rooms were most likely outfitted in American Empire style, while the later Victorian period found massive, Renaissance Revival furniture particularly well suited to the din-

"The dining room should be light and airy. If possible it should have a pleasant outlook and a window through which the morning sunlight will enter.... Paper the walls with warm tints and have both dado and frieze. Have an inlaid wood, oiled, stained or painted floor on which rugs may be used or dispensed with according to taste. The window drapery should be in deep, rich colors. The chairs should be chosen square, solid styles and upholstered in embossed or plain leather. The dining-table should be low, square or bevel-cornered, and when not in use should be covered with a cloth corresponding in shade to the window drapery.... The sideboard should be of high, massive style, with shelves and racks for glassware and pieces of china. There was a time when the dining room looked like a picture gallery; but the prevailing fashion now confines the number of pictures to two or three small fruit pieces and one or two plaques of still life."

Richard A. Wells, A.M.
Manners, Culture and Dress of the Best American Society, *1891*

ing room. Eastlake furniture was popular during the 1880s and 1890s, as were factory-produced golden oak sets or pieces in the Arts and Crafts style, which were in use during the 1890s and early 1900s.

Dining room tables were round, rectangular, or square, and many of the tables turned out during the late 1800s had extensions or leaves, which could be added to make the table considerably larger. The accompanying chairs were frequently straight-backed and an armchair was common at both the head and foot of the table.

Sideboards were the most popular accessory item in furnishing the dining room, and were in fact thought by some to be a necessity. Many examples were extremely large and ornate, providing room not only for dishes, linens, and silverware, but also shelves on which to display fine china, crystal, decorative glass, and sterling silver or silver plate.

The formality that was a hallmark of the Victorian dining room never wavered throughout the nineteenth century. There was, however, a fine line between tasteful decor and a vulgar or ostentatious display of goods. Refinement was the key word, and while we may look back and see an over-abundance of items displayed and used, Victorians did practice restraint to avoid overstepping their bounds in the proper Victorian dining room.

Creating a Victorian Dining Room

Who wouldn't welcome the opportunity to step back in time and enjoy a sumptuous meal, spirited conversation, and the warm, comfortable surroundings of the nineteenth-century dining room?

Today we have the wherewithal to re-create the rich beauty of this Victorian setting, whether in High Style or with a toned-down approach. Whether this room will serve as an area in which to lavishly entertain or simply to play host to intimate family gatherings, a potpourri of ideas will entice you to shape a Victorian dining room of your own.

If the splendor of the Gilded Age is your passion, the Victorian High Style dining room will be a true delight. This room almost—but not quite—mirrored the excess found in the Victorian parlor. A tempered hand was everywhere apparent in the dining room, achieving just the right combination of ornamentation and respectable good taste. Likewise, today's High Style dining room is a carefully orchestrated blend of color and pattern that evokes pleasant emotions, while a tasteful arrangement of furnishings and accessories adds a goodly dose of opulence.

In contrast, a romance-inspired dining room is apt to reflect the simpler designs associated with Eastlake's reform movement, still following earlier dictates that called for warmth and comfort, but making full use of William Morris wallpapers with stylized floral or foliage patterns.

In homes with a modern, eclectic, or country theme, subtle nuances can introduce Victorian charm in small but significant ways. Quaint accessories or a piece or two of vintage furniture are all that's needed to warm up a contemporary decor.

The various historical aspects of the Victorian dining room—wall treatment, floor covering, ceiling embellishments, lighting, window dressing, furniture, and decorative accessories and collectibles—were all equally important in achieving just the right look. Rather than vying for attention, these disparate elements were to complement one another, thereby defining the well-appointed dining room.

WALL TREATMENTS

Covering the largest expanse in the dining room, the wall treatment reflected a choice of colors around which the rest of the room was planned.

During the early years of the Victorian period, household experts recommended the use of somber colors such as gray or light brown. By mid-century, warm, rich shades were favored, and various tints of red, such as crimson and claret, were overwhelmingly popular. This practice of assigning warm colors to the dining room continued, and wallpaper was frequently the treatment of choice.

Prior to the introduction of the tripartite wall in the 1870s, wallpaper was applied from ceiling to baseboard (as it had been in the parlor), occasionally incorporating a border or protective wooden chair rail. Popular pat-

Recalling mid-nineteenth-century Victorian style, this dining room has been treated to walls papered in warm tones and a floral-patterned wall-to-wall carpet.

terns included fresco papers (giving a sectional look employing flowers, landscapes, and so on), which in fact made the wall appear as if it had been painted with a mural.

During the late 1870s a horizontal division of wall space (dado or wainscot, field, and frieze) was as appropriate in the dining

room as it was in the parlor, and critics voiced the opinion that these two rooms should complement each other, given their close proximity in many homes. For example, a citrine yellow and peacock blue color scheme in the parlor (used in tripartite fashion) was reversed in the dining room so that colors flowed from one room to the next.

Wallpapers used in the dining room during the late 1870s and into the 1890s were often based on patterns popularized by Arts and Crafts reformists William Morris and Walter Crane of England, and exhibited small, abstract floral designs, foliage, birds, and so forth. Although Morris had designed three wallpaper patterns (*Trellis, Daisy,* and *Pomegranate*) by the mid-1860s , it was another dozen years before most Americans became familiar with his work, via the 1876 Centennial Exposition in Philadelphia. By then Morris had added to his portfolio of designs, and the American public was captivated by his fresh patterns, his use of color, and the distinct naturalistic overtones of his work. These romantic wallpapers were first hand-printed and then later machine-made in stunning colors created by combining primary and secondary hues. The results were beautiful yellows, earthy terra-cotta, a deep, peacock blue, olive green, old gold, and Pompeiian red.

Wooden wainscoting had also been a popular wall treatment in the late Victorian period and continued to be so through the turn of the century.

In many households the call to simplify interiors (especially during the 1890s) resulted in scaled-back dining room walls, including a wallpaper and frieze (but no dado) or a wainscot and papered wall minus the frieze. In more formal homes (Colonial Revival styles), wallpapers with classical motifs

A stunning example of the tripartite wall treatment, this Victorian-inspired dining room has been treated to an elaborate wood wainscot, a wallpaper field, and an unusual frieze. Gleaming wood and earthy colors, along with stenciled ceiling and ample appointments, make this room elegant yet welcoming.

"There is nothing like individual taste in these matters (of decoration); but a few hints will be acceptable.... In your Dining-Room...the paper should be rich and warm in tone, without staring patterns, and the cornice, and moldings massive....The general effect should be that of substantial comfort."

Alexander V. Hamilton
The Household
Cyclopaedia of Practical Receipts
and Daily Wants, *1873*

appeared once again, but followers of the reform movements continued to rely on the small floral and nonrealistic geometric designs of Morris and others to decorate the all-important dining room. Warm wall colors (claret, olive, blue, brown) were still paired with lighter shades (salmon, buff, orange, tan) exhibited in a frieze.

During the 1890s and early 1900s there were few "incorrect" ways of dressing the dining room walls. Personal choice and the architectural style of the house were the most common determining factors.

Today's formal High Style dining room can be enhanced with the warm colors associated with this space throughout much of the Victorian era. Strong, dark furnishings are complemented by a wallpaper with large floral designs, scenic papers, or a wallpaper with two-toned stripes of color. Papering the entire wall in a single pattern is in keeping with the formal style (reminiscent of revival periods); a rich-toned wainscot in combination with wallpaper or paint can achieve the same elegant effect.

The romantic Victorian dining room, recalling reform movement styles in vogue during the later part of the century, can be resplendent when treated with a tripartite division of wall space. William Morris–inspired wallpapers are especially apropos, and many of his patterns are being reproduced today. A sturdy, embossed Lincrusta paper featured as a dado and painted a darker shade than the rest of the wall is another striking alternative. It's also a practical choice, as the dark, textured Lincrusta will hide scuffs from chairs or passersby.

If a simplified style is more to your liking, a wainscot with a wraparound plate rail and wallpaper extending from rail to ceiling is a desirable treatment. Other possibilities

A simplified version of the traditional horizontal division of wall space, this two-part treatment with wainscoting and wallpaper is Victorian in spirit and decorative by design. The use of lighter colors contributes to the cheerful atmosphere of the room.

include using wallpaper and frieze, or painting your walls in a warm shade and then accenting them with a frieze or border.

In the dining room with modern, eclectic, or country overtones, your wall treatment can introduce subtle Victorian taste by way of an impressive wainscot, a nineteenth-century-inspired tint (such as gray, lilac, or blue), or a wallpaper carefully chosen to evoke the spirit of the Victorian age.

FLOORING

Before hardwood floors made their debut in the 1870s, the dining room was treated to carpeting with large floral or foliage patterns or with geometric designs. A drugget (a coarse, woven cloth) was frequently placed under the table and chairs—atop the carpeting—to protect the room-sized rug from spills during formal dinners.

The popularity of hardwood floors in the parlor and dining room coincided with the 1870s American publication of Charles Eastlake's book, *Hints on Household Taste*. He told readers "...the practice of entirely covering up the floor, and thus leaving no evidence of its material, is contrary to the first principles of decorative art, which require that the nature of construction, so far as possible, should always be revealed, or at least indicated, by the ornament which it bears." In other words, the natural wood material comprising the floor was to be appreciated, and if it could be made beautiful or ornamental with various designs or patterns, so much the better.

Parquetry, long considered a decorative art form in France, was recommended by Eastlake. Design critics agreed that a parquet border extending a few feet from the wall, around the perimeter of the room, was both artistic and practical. In this way, observed Eastlake, a quality carpet could be purchased in a smaller size and would be adaptable to other rooms if need be.

A full, handcrafted parquet wood floor was very costly and was found mainly in the homes of the well-to-do. Middle-class Victorians, on the other hand, made use of factory-produced parquet borders to line the dining room, or "wood carpet" (strips of hardwood on a heavy backing) could be bought to cover an entire room, thus creating the look of hardwood without the expense. Parquet borders or flooring were available in a variety of designs during the last quarter of the nineteenth century, including the ever-popular herringbone pattern.

Painting or staining a softwood dining room floor in imitation of hardwood was also a popular practice.

Once the floor was embellished or stained, an Oriental rug often assumed a place of honor in the center of the room. Eastlake highly recommended Orientals but advised care in selecting designs to avoid introducing an excess of color that would overwhelm the harmonious blend of furnishings, wall treatment, and so on. While hand-made Oriental rugs from the Far East were prized for their craftsmanship and superb quality, machine-made examples were far less costly. It was these mass-produced rugs that were on display in the majority of Victorian dining rooms.

In addition to Oriental designs, rugs with mosaic patterns were acceptable, provided the colors were not too strong, and Wiltons (cut-pile) and Brussels (looped-pile) carpets with simple floral patterns were commonly used. Deep shades were preferred, since the rug served as a backdrop in the Victorian dining room.

Today's Victorian-inspired dining room can benefit from the excellent selection of carpeting and area rugs available. In addition, hardwood flooring in stunning designs combining a variety of woods has enjoyed renewed interest and popularity.

A formal High Style dining room can be beautiful when treated to luxurious wall-to-wall carpeting. If a long-lasting, stain-resistant wool carpet is beyond your means, a synthetic nylon is the next best choice, for it wears well, has a rich look, and is available in a wide selection of colors. A solid-color carpeting, whether it stands alone or is dressed with an area rug laid under the table, will enhance the formal setting and add a welcoming touch.

A patterned carpet with large floral or geometric designs can also lend Victorian ambience to a formal setting, especially if the floor treatment is combined with subtle paint on dining room walls. A tapestry or needle-point rug sets off a parquet or simpler hard-wood floor particularly well.

The romantic High Style dining room is the perfect spot for an Oriental rug. Neutral colors will blend nicely with patterned walls, or your area rug can display the deep shades from which walls take their cue.

An Oriental area rug can also be the per-fect vintage touch in a modern or eclectic dining room and blends nicely in a country setting as well. Depending upon your floor

A model of good taste, this sumptuous dining room is made warm and inviting with carpet bedecked in a floral and foliage motif. Victorian ambience is created here through the use of pattern, color, and distinctive archi-tectural details.

plan and whether or not you have a separate dining room, creative measures may be called for. For example, if your dining space is an extension of a carpeted living room, consider placing an Oriental or other decorative rug under the table to clearly define this space. If your dining area is adjacent to the kitchen, a hardwood floor can add an elegant touch in an otherwise casual setting.

CEILINGS

As one of two rooms in which Victorians entertained, the dining room often sported a ceiling embellished with tinted paints, medal-lions, or wallpaper, just as in the parlor. Gilded cornices were favored during the mid-century period to add a formal, rich look, and decorative sunken panels could be used to create a domelike effect (referred to as a coffered ceiling) for those who could afford it. The ceiling may also have been ornamented with a mural (called a fresco) or stenciled with an eye-catching design.

During the last quarter of the nineteenth century, decorative metal ceilings were in vogue and were less costly than an elabo-rately plastered ceiling. Metal ceilings were frequently found in the kitchen and bath-room but were put to use in many middle-class dining rooms as well. Praised for their practical as well as decorative qualities, pressed-tin ceiling panels were fire-retar-dant, easy to clean, and considered sanitary in an era plagued by disease and the spread of germs. From an ornamental viewpoint, metal ceilings were available in a wide variety of designs that echoed elaborate Gothic, Rococo, or Renaissance styles. Sold in two-foot (0.6m) -wide sections of varying length, the tin panels could easily be nailed into place and were often sold in kits. A sin-

Above: Substantial and almost masculine in appearance, this coffered ceiling with a center dome adds architectural interest to the room.

Left: Befitting a king—or perhaps a Victorian robber baron—this lavish dining room has been finished with a stunning ceiling fresco. Generally reserved for the homes of the well-to-do, this is an impressive example of Victoriana at its best.

gle pattern was used on the large expanse of the ceiling and then a trim or molding was placed around the perimeter. A decorative cornice completed this ceiling treatment.

The formal dining room decorated in today's Victorian Revival style can be enhanced by any number of ceiling decorations. Most simply, the ceiling can be painted in a lighter shade of the color featured on the walls. This is especially appropriate where an illusion of height is preferred, as a lightly tinted ceiling tends to visually increase space.

A reproduction center medallion adds an elegant touch in a formal dining room and serves as an ornate backdrop for a stunning chandelier. Gilt cornices or delicate stenciled designs strategically placed around the perimeter of the ceiling draw the eyes upward, add a feeling of richness, and indicate careful attention to detail.

In the romance-inspired dining room, a ceiling paper can work in tandem with the paper on the wall to create a glorious opulence. Papers specifically re-created for Victorian-style ceilings are being produced and can be matched with corresponding wallpapers.

In more subtle romantic spirit, the ceiling can be painted, a softly patterned paper can be applied and brought down the wall to a decorative plate rail, or a decorative pressed-tin ceiling can be installed. Several manufacturers produce metal ceiling panels today, some with a brass finish, and metal cornices are available as well. The vintage charm of a metal ceiling is especially welcome in older homes where the dining room ceiling may be in poor shape.

In small dining areas with an eclectic, modern, or country style, the softness of Victoriana can be incorporated by stenciling around the edge of the ceiling or painting the ceiling in a light or pastel shade.

LIGHTING

Like the Victorian parlor, the nineteenth-century dining room was often lit with a combination of light fixtures, including several kerosene lamps, candles, and later gasoliers and electroliers (hanging gas or electric light fixtures).

Early chandeliers, which supported numerous candles, were often quite elaborate, while later brass or cast-iron kerosene fixtures were less fussy. The kerosene hanging fixtures incorporated chains or pulleys in their design so that the oil could be replen-

ished, and then the fixture, with anywhere from two to four lamps, could be raised back into place. Such hanging fixtures were most often located over the center of the table, three feet (0.9m) or so above the tabletop.

Wall fixtures or sconces were common in the dining room, as were kerosene lamps with shades and, of course, a goodly supply of candles. The kerosene lamps and candlesticks in ornate silver, silver plate, brass, or glass were placed on the dining room table, mantel, or sideboard.

As the century progressed, urban areas took full advantage of new fuels and sources of power. The gasolier replaced the kerosene hanging fixture, and later the electric lamp was put to use. The Art Nouveau Movement introduced hanging fixtures with breathtaking art-glass shades, and the Arts and Crafts Movement brought brass fixtures with beautiful slag-glass shades. (Slag glass, created in a variety of colors, has an opaque, almost milky, appearance.)

The formal High Style dining room in today's home is the perfect setting for a brilliant chandelier. Add elegance and create an intimate atmosphere by placing distinctive candlesticks on the table or about the room, where they shed flattering light on the dinner scene.

Soft lighting in the dining room was important in creating the proper atmosphere. The mirror over the mantel reflects subtle lighting from the beautiful hanging fixture while the small lamps on the table cast a warm glow with their fringed fabric shades.

A romantic dining room harkens back to the Victorian period of gasoliers and electroliers. An iron or brass hanging lamp with a frosted or etched-glass shade is the ideal fixture in a room decked out in warmly patterned wallpaper or a deep shade of paint. A stunning art-glass fixture pays tribute to the Aesthetic Movement and introduces just a touch of the eclectic in a room noted for tasteful restraint. An Arts and Crafts fixture blends well in the dining room that features furnishings or accessories of the same style, such as a Mission oak table and chairs, and sideboards laden with pottery pieces.

In the dining room where other decorating schemes take center stage, a Victorian-style fixture can introduce nineteenth-century spirit in a bold or subtle way, and candlelight improves every setting, no matter what the decorative style may be.

Making decisions regarding lighting fixtures can be confusing when you're trying to choose between authentic pieces or reproductions. In opting to invest in nineteenth-century lighting fixtures, seek the advice of an antiques dealer or restoration expert who specializes in this area. To the untrained eye, a vintage lighting fixture is virtually impossible to assess.

WINDOW TREATMENTS

The window dressings in the Victorian dining room were often every bit as elaborate as those found in the parlor. Layering the dining room windows with shutters or a shade, lace panels, and a floor-length curtain or drapery, then finishing the look with a lambrequin, or decorative valance, was customary during the early Victorian period. Such window dressings, with the outer drapery fashioned from a rich fabric in a color

Above: The lavish architectural details and elegant furnishings of this High Style Victorian dining room call for a luxurious window dressing. Full-length curtains puddle at the floor and a sensuous valance of soft scallops tempers the bold lines of the furniture.

Left: Graced with beautiful stained-glass windows, this Victorian dining room benefits from a simple window dressing of handsome curtains held back with elegant cords and tassels.

that complemented the deep tones of the room, spoke of good taste and financial means. Velvet curtains in a handsome wine color with elaborate accessories, such as gold tassels and fringes, were the ultimate fashion statement.

With romance and an appreciation of nature brought to the forefront of the late Victorian era by various reform movements, window dressing became less stylized. Layers were removed until dining room windows were left shuttered and draped in delicate lace panels. A corresponding swag completed the light and airy effect.

By the turn of the century, critics were calling for careful selections in choosing curtains for the dining room. A heavy drapery would make a small room appear even smaller, while a light window dressing would get lost in a large room. Good judgment was called for, with simple, tasteful treatments—not garishly overdone windows—prevailing.

In decorating today's formal High Style dining room, by all means, dress your windows! Tempered by the modern taste for trimmed-down fashion, lace panels and a sumptuous drapery of deep-toned velvet, elegantly patterned brocade, or exquisite satin enhance the stately feel of the room. Top it off with a valance for a polished look or a swag for a softer touch. A jabot, a fall of fabric cascading from either a valance or a swag, can be added for decorative flair. Fringed tassels or elegant rope cords, used to loop your drapery back during the day, are a luxurious final touch to the formal window.

A romantic dining room treated to a sensuous wallpaper and perhaps an Oriental rug is the perfect setting for a soft touch of lace, shutters, or perhaps a dressy balloon shade, which creates an attractive, puffed display of fabric when raised. Shutters can be painted to match the walls or stained to blend with a handsome wood wainscot. Shutters have the added attraction of offering the illusion of architectural embellishment in a dining room that has no notable woodwork.

The old house featuring art-glass windows in the dining room benefits from the glorious colors that stream into the room during the day. By visiting an architectural salvage emporium or one of the larger antiques shows you can uncover one of these treasured relics and claim it for your very own. Secure it in front of a plain-glass window (with hooks and a sturdy chain), and you can enjoy the same artistic effect that graced many a late-nineteenth-century home. A simple shutter or lace panel on the

"Besides the regular dining-room furniture, tables, chairs, sideboard, and serving table, the addition of a plate rail or rack for plates, pitchers, and other decorative china objects, and of a china cabinet with glass doors for displaying the best china, help to give a room character and beauty. The effect of these articles will be very much heightened if the wall coverings are in solid colors.... The color scheme of the dining room should preferably be in cheerful tones, as blues, yellows, or reds, according to the amount of light the room receives."

Sidney Morse
Household Discoveries, *1908*

bottom portion of the window is all that's called for to complete these colorful, eye-catching windows.

Other decorating styles—modern, eclectic, or country—can borrow from the past to bring a hint of Victoriana into the present day. Whether dressed with elaborate drapes and trim or sporting only a subtle touch of lace, a nineteenth century–inspired window dressing can soften the spare look of a modern setting. Shutters are ideal in any dining room where a simplified treatment is preferred, as are fabric shades in muted colors or with soft, floral designs.

FURNISHINGS

During the early nineteenth century, when only the grand homes of the affluent had a separate dining room, most middle-class families combined an eating area with a sitting room. Their dining furniture often included a drop-leaf table and factory-made Hitchcock chairs (named after Lambert Hitchcock, who established the first chair factory in the 1820s), which were slat-backed, embellished with stenciled designs, and sported rush, wood, or cane seats. Meanwhile, a wealthy few turned to the cabinetmaker, who may have created a beautiful Gothic-style table and chairs for the dining room or perhaps a rosewood table, which was often accompanied by Rococo Revival–style balloon-back side chairs.

As more and more people experienced prosperity, homes were built at a furious pace, and separate rooms for dining and entertaining became commonplace. Furniture manufacturers responded by turning out dining room suites just as they were creating the popular parlor sets. By this mid-century period Renaissance Revival style was all the rage, and ponderous tables and sideboards fresh from the factory filled middle-class dining rooms. These suites, usually made of walnut, had tables that were round, square, or rectangular, with extension leaves that could easily triple the size of the table. With assorted decorative veneer panels, roundels, and scrollwork, they were well ornamented and most impressive.

Dining room chairs of this same style were generally straight-back, embellished with carved head crests or pediments and with plush, upholstered seats.

The massive and masculine Renaissance Revival sideboard was the most ornate furnishing in the Victorian dining room. With some examples reaching to heights of eight feet (2.4m), the storage space on the bottom, which was hidden by carved doors (fruit, nuts, and animal carvings were common), was home to glassware and china. Drawers with carved-wood pulls were for linen and silverware, and a beautiful marble top could be used to show off special items. Extending upward several feet, a lavish backboard with shelves (and often a mirror) was dressed with additional moldings, applied ornaments, and a carved pediment. The shelves displayed choice possessions, and the mirror served to reflect soft light across the room.

With the introduction of Eastlake furniture in the late 1870s, the call to simplify designs altered—but did not eliminate—fancywork. Eastlake dining suites (tables, chairs, and a sideboard) were rectilinear in shape and decorated with incised lines, applied brackets, and nature-inspired carvings. In addition, recessed burled veneer panels, marble tops, and decorative shelves and mirrors were often featured on Eastlake sideboards. Early examples of Eastlake furnishings were crafted in walnut, but as

this wood grew scarce during the last quarter of the century oak, cherry, chestnut, and ash were called into use.

Renaissance Revival and Eastlake-style furnishings predominated in the Victorian dining room well into the 1880s and 1890s, respectively, and factory-made golden oak sets were popular during the 1890s and into the twentieth century. Especially at home in rural areas or small dwellings where function was the primary concern, golden oak tables, chairs, sideboards, and china cabinets were as sturdy and practical as they were lovely.

Reflecting the scaled-back approach to decorating called for during the late nineteenth century, this dining room is outfitted with a handsome table and the all-important sideboard—a prerequisite in this room devoted to entertaining.

In addition, many middle-class Victorians found the light wood finish a pleasant change from the sober, dark woods that had presided in the dining room for decades. Whether in a simple, straightforward design or embellished with paw feet and ornamental trim, oak furnishings were quite popular in the dining room designed for a light and airy feel.

In outfitting today's High Style dining room, if space will allow, a handsome table, chairs, and sideboard are a necessity. For a more formal look, turn to traditional revival styles such as Renaissance Revival or consider one of the Colonial Revival styles that appeared during the late nineteenth century such as Queen Anne or Chippendale. A romantic High Style dining room, inspired by the warm colors and sensuous designs of the last thirty years of the century, is ideally furnished in the Eastlake style or with golden oak—the more ornate the better. Simpler furnishings sans gingerbread trim are perfect for a cottage or bungalow. Remember, simplicity can be elegant.

Other decorating styles can be enhanced in the dining room by incorporating Victorian style or substyle furnishings to a lesser degree. An otherwise modern setting can be striking when a handsome vintage sideboard takes center stage.

The mix-and-match eclectic room may incorporate a nineteenth-century table and chairs or accessory piece, and the country dining room may temper a rustic air with the soft touch of wicker chairs. The patina of a scrubbed pine table can be complemented by rustic Adirondack chairs that recall the Victorians' love of nature.

When searching for antique dining room chairs, it can be difficult to find a matched set. Using several different chairs of the same style around the table can solve this problem when they are dressed in the same fabric or stained the same shade—thus giving them a unified appearance.

Whether you choose to look for authentic nineteenth-century pieces or reproductions, the source directory in the back of this book will help you locate shops.

DECORATIVE ACCESSORIES AND COLLECTIBLES

The Victorian dining room in full regalia wore the badge of good social standing. Handsome furnishings, the tastefully decorated shell of the room, and carefully dressed windows were accessorized with various decorative and functional objects that spoke of wealth, refinement, and a comfortable knowledge of the rules of etiquette.

Subtleties such as silk cords on the curtains, the latest fashion in wall hangings, an abundance of fresh flowers, and select greenery were accompanied by quality linens, fine china, glassware, and a profusion of silver. The best of the best was everywhere apparent in the formal Victorian dining room.

Linens embellished with lace softened the masculinity of massive dining room tables and created an elegant backdrop on which to present the lavish meal. Fine napkins accompanied each place setting and delicate doilies were often placed underneath special objects displayed on the sideboard or mantel. When the table was not in use, a decorative table scarf was usually in place, since a bare tabletop was considered dull.

During the early nineteenth century, looms especially designed for lace making created affordable and stunning laces. Middle-class Victorians could lay claim to what was once within reach of only the wealthy, and a lace tablecloth became a symbol of prosperi-

ty. It was, in fact, an important part of the trousseau for the mid-Victorian bride-to-be. During later years, linen tablecloths and napkins with a damask weave were commonly used in the dining room, as were table coverings combining linen with fringe or lace, which was used as trimwork or featured as an inset in the center of the cloth.

Well-to-do Victorians had a love of European laces that bordered on obsession. In many a Victorian home, however, the mistress, long-skilled in needlework, could purchase the fine lace of her choice and lovingly stitch it to a imported linen tablecloth, thus creating a work of art.

Gracing the sideboard, as well as the table when set for entertaining, were the fine china and glassware that the Victorians were so very proud of. The wealthy could afford the more costly British and European china, but the majority of middle-class Victorians found merit in white ironstone (made first in Britain and later in the United States). Ironstone embellished with a blue transfer printed design, commonly called "Flow Blue," dressed many a Victorian dinner table and was popular throughout the nineteenth century. Flow Blue, as well as other transfer wares, was created in a several-step process. A copper plate bearing the pattern or design was coated with a cobalt pigment, and tissue paper was then applied to the design. This in turn was carefully placed on plates and other

---

This lovely table setting combines fine china with striking blue stemware. As the perfect finishing touch, a centerpiece of fresh flowers presides over the table.

dishes to transfer the design, and a glaze was applied before the object was fired. The result was an underglaze transfer print.

The decorative designs of Flow Blue mirrored the changing styles during the Victorian period as dishware was adorned with Oriental motifs, naturalistic floral and foliage patterns, and later stylized Art Nouveau designs.

Regardless of the type of china chosen for use, the formal dinner called for a staggering number of service pieces depending upon the menu. Items in common use at the Victorian table included dinner plates, soup plates and bowls, butter dishes, bone dishes, salt dishes, dessert plates, coffee cups, custard cups, platters, covered vegetable dishes, chop plates, serving dishes, berry bowls, covered casseroles and tureens, gravy boats and trays, sauce boats, spoon trays, pickle and cheese dishes, ladles, pitchers, and compotes. Separate tea services were used for afternoon entertaining.

If the dining room table was not decked out in fine china, then exquisite glassware—or a combination of china and glass—was used. After molded, pressed glass manufacture began in the mid-nineteenth century, many of the objects generally made of china were routinely produced in glass as well, along with wine glasses, goblets, punch bowls, celery vases, cake stands, salt and pepper shakers, tiny salt cellars, sugar shakers, castor bottles, and decanters.

Crystal or clear glass was made in abundance and in a variety of patterns, many pieces embellished with engravings or etched designs. During the late Victorian period, patterned, colored glass was in vogue, and beautiful items were created in blues, greens, yellows, reds, and the ever-popular cranberry color. Cranberry glass was produced

Small touches of Victoriana add big impact. A romantic white tablecloth is the perfect backdrop for this eye-catching display of mix-and-match tableware. Elegant embroidered napkins accessorized with silver rings and flowers reflect creative effort with smashing results.

by numerous companies for many years, and among the more popular decorative items Victoriana buffs search for today are candlesticks, compotes, decanters, rose bowls, pitchers, and vases.

By the 1880s, opaque or satin art glass with appealing names like Peachblow, Amberian, or Burmese glass became fashionable, as well as brilliant, cut-glass tableware. With the Art Nouveau Movement came stunning iridescent glass in deep shades of gold, blue, or purple, and shortly after the turn of the century, what we commonly refer to as carnival glass was being mass-produced in imitation of the more costly iridescent glass created by the likes of Louis Tiffany.

Silver and silver plate were among the most cherished dining room accessories during the Victorian era. While only the wealthy could display or make use of costly silver pieces turned out by notable manufacturers such as Gorham & Company, the Charles Louis Tiffany Company, or Reed & Barton, the introduction of silver plate during the mid-nineteenth century made silver available to one and all. Silver plating involved coating a base metal with silver, and quality was determined by the amount of silver found in the base metal as well as the number of electroplated coatings that had been applied. In typical Victorian fashion, silver and silver plate items, such as flatware and decorative accessories, were embellished in innumerable ways. Items we are no longer familiar with (such as cracker spoons, berry forks, waffle knives, or cheese scoops) were brought to the dining table, and the proper Victorian's knowledge of their purpose (as well as following through with correct use) indicated that the individual was well schooled in etiquette—a hallmark of moral standing and a measure of success in life.

The table was set with a combination (once again depending on the menu) of spoons, forks, knives, ladles, sifters, servers, and so on. A complete listing of items would undoubtedly go on for several pages, but a sampling includes a variety of spoons for berries, coffee, dessert, gravy, ice cream, jelly, nuts, olives, salt, soup, and tea. Forks were designed for serving or eating cheese, fish, dessert, salad, oysters, pickles, sardines,

"The table-cloth should be of the finest quality, ornamented with lace embroidery, if desired; but the latest edict of fashion precludes the introduction of any colored materials that do not wash.... The room may be lighted with either white or colored candles or lamps.... Decorations should always be arranged in such a manner that they will not interfere with the guests' view of one another. At present the preference is for low dishes of flowers of delicate perfume; all those which have a strong fragrance, such as tube-roses, etc., should be avoided, as the odor is apt to become oppressive in a warm room."

Mrs. John A. Logan
The Home Manual, *1890*

toast, and vegetables. Knives were needed for butter, cake, cheese, fish, jelly, slicing ice cream, or serving pie. Carving knives and forks, assorted servers for asparagus, fried oysters, and Saratoga chips, and miscellaneous items such as tongs (for sugar and ice), butter picks, and scoops were all necessary in the Victorian dining room.

Popular accessory pieces included silver-plated cake stands, call bells (to ring for a servant), castors (a stand containing cruets or glass condiment bottles), elegant coffee and tea services, crumb trays and scrapers (to brush the table before dessert was served), elaborate fruit stands, napkin rings, nutcrackers, picks, spoon holders, pitchers, wine stands, and so forth.

All the aforementioned items, so wonderfully new to the Victorians, are today our beloved antiques and collectibles. Not only do we hunt antiques shows, estate sales, and auctions in search of vintage lace and linens and antique china, glassware, or silver to set a Victorian table or to display the beauty of these pieces, but we delight in the charm of objects so inventive and we revel in the Victorians' never-ending attention to the most minute detail.

In today's Victorian-inspired dining room, be creative and personalize with accessories and collectibles to achieve the effect you desire. Since vintage tableware is often difficult to locate in complete sets, consider mixing and matching, with a color scheme in mind and patterns that complement one another. The results can be beautiful in a formal setting as well as in the room that features select hints of Victoriana.

With your dining room decorated, plan an elegant dinner, select your menu, invite the guests, set the table, and enjoy the flavor of Victorian life.

———

His and Hers

The Library and the Sitting Room

———

Welcome to the inner sanctum of the Victorian home. Enter the library, "his" domain, where the man of the house could retreat for quiet relaxation, for the pleasure of a good book, to conduct business with associates, or to socialize with his contemporaries. "Her" refuge, the sitting room, was a comfy, special place, a haven of domesticity. Here, time was spent with family or devoted to light reading, needlework, or arts and crafts. Relaxation, conversation with a loved one, or soothing, rhythmic handiwork occupied the treasured moments spent in the peace of the sitting room.

———

These rooms, considered private, were rarely subject to the scrutiny of callers or guests. Solid comfort was paramount in furnishings as well as the cherished mementos and objects that found a home in these rooms.

———

Retreat to your own sanctuary, enjoy a cup of tea, and read on as we explore the private worlds of the mistress and master of the Victorian home.

———

The very essence of Victorian style, this massive library combines all the comforts of home: built-in bookcases, warm colors for quiet repose, tasteful floor coverings, ample furnishings, and, of course, books. Note, too, how the deep shades of color have been continued across the ceiling with a handsome wallpaper.

The History of the Library

During the early Victorian period it was a fortunate family indeed that could set aside a room for a library. Home culture—instructing children in all aspects of polite society and the world around them—as well as self-culture—the moral, intellectual, and physical pursuits that enhance good citizenship and social standing—called for the study of numerous books. Pleasurable reading material, as well as instructional manuals that aided in self-improvement, were found in the majority of middle-class Victorian homes by the mid-nineteenth century. With the Victorians' insatiable thirst for knowledge, it is no wonder these precious books were assigned a place of honor in the nineteenth-century home. A library in some form was considered an important part of the household and, in fact, became a status symbol—a measure of success and a barometer of social standing and worldliness.

A distinctly masculine domain throughout the nineteenth century, the library was decorated in somber shades befitting a place of quiet study or retreat. Furnishings were massive and comfortable, as well as serviceable, and the variety of pieces typically found in the library included upholstered armchairs, footstools, a sofa or settee, side chairs, assorted tables, a desk or two, and masses of bookcases. In the homes of the affluent, walls were lined with beautiful built-in bookcases with protective glass doors. Rich woodwork enhanced the masculine overtones of the library and it was not unusual for walls to be paneled or wainscoted with deep oak, cherry, or mahogany. In smaller homes freestanding bookcases were used in place of built-in shelves.

While the library's ornamentation was associated with manly pursuits such as hunting, smoking, business, and maintaining family records and ledgers, and thus devoid of feminine frills, it was no less attractive or appealing than other rooms in the house. The very richness of the books created a decorative element and the warm colors employed throughout the room made it inviting and cocoonlike.

During the later Victorian period, the deep colors typically found in the public areas of the house (the entrance hall, parlor, and dining room) spilled over into the library, and walls were painted or papered in the popular reds, greens, or blues. Carpeting covered the floors while a formal dressing presided over windows.

If the middle-class home was without a separate library, the sitting room usually included a desk or a secretary for writing letters and keeping household accounts, and also bookcases to house the family's collection of biographies, popular fiction, poetry, history, encyclopedias, travel works, and books devoted to science, nature, deportment, and drama.

With the introduction of Arts and Crafts bungalow architecture before the turn of the century, floor plans included more open spaces and built-in shelving in the living room, which often did away with the need for a library in these smaller homes.

The Victorian concept of devoting space to private places within the home lingers today. Past and present day—we share the need to have a quiet corner where we can retreat with a good book or our own secret thoughts.

> *"It is not too much to say that every man owes it to himself, no less than his family, to provide a home; a spot around which he may gather his dear ones for counsel and instruction. Such a home is incomplete without one apartment, too often little regarded, which is a library."*
>
> *Henry Hudson Holly*
> Holly's Country Seats, *1863*

Creating a Victorian Library

The modern counterpart of the Victorian library is the den or home office. Whether you have the luxury of setting aside an entire room as a library, in traditional Victorian fashion, or must combine such an area with equipment to meet present-day needs, borrowing the best of Victoriana can create a setting that is both functional and fashionable. Yes, high tech can comfortably coexist with nineteenth-century style.

As we explore the Victorian library, many of the elements that created this inviting room—the wall treatment, floor coverings, ceiling decor, lighting, window dressing, furniture, and decorative accessories and collectibles—can be adapted for modern use. Suggestions are offered for creating a High Style library as well as details that introduce Victorian style into a no-nonsense work space. Above all, keep Victorian spirit in mind—then and now, this a very personal space.

"A room specially furnished as a library is not possible in all homes. It is not only a great luxury where it can be afforded, but has also an important educational influence. If a room can be spared for the purpose no great expense is required to furnish a library attractively, as the books themselves, if properly arranged, go far toward giving the room a habitable look."

Sidney Morse
Household Discoveries, *1908*

WALL TREATMENTS

Early Victorian–era libraries were painted in subtle shades such as gray or blue, and as wainscoting became popular, the bottom portion of the walls was often enhanced with dark wood panels that created a rich, baronial setting. Any library of substantial size had bookcases lining one or more walls, and a fireplace was included to warm the room as well as provide a cozy spot in which to read or relax.

When interior design took on the colors and patterns inspired by Eastlake, the library was tastefully painted or papered in deep

The rusty brown shade that adorns these library walls was considered to be restful. Victorian influence is also seen here in the glass-enclosed bookcases, the hardwood floor with area rug, and the bamboo shade at the window, conveying just a hint of exotica.

shades of red, green, or even purple. Colors were carefully chosen so that walls would not be so dark that it was difficult to provide

"The walls [in the library] should be hung with rich colors—not so dark as to make it difficult to light the room sufficiently in the evening, but it must not be too light, or we shall lose the feeling of repose we most want. A carpet of Pompeiian red is both rich and cheerful. The room should be furnished with broad easy chairs, low tables for books and periodicals, and bookshelves arranged at a convenient height, and so any book may be reached without stretching or mounting on a chair or stool. Soft rugs, foot-rests, a mantel mirror and a few mantel ornaments complete the furniture. It is quite in vogue to hang curtains on rods in front of the book-cases. Curtains of raw silks or Turcoman are used for window draperies."

Richard A. Wells, A.M.
Manners, Culture and Dress of the Best American Society, *1891*

sufficient light; yet too light a color would diminish the feeling of relaxation the library was noted for.

By the turn of the century, the Arts and Crafts Movement called for library walls painted or papered in restful colors such as reds or browns.

A room devoted to books and relaxation may today be dressed in subtle shades such as gray or salmon to evoke the Gothic Revival influence that was everywhere apparent in the early Victorian library. Built-in bookcases, paneled walls, or a wainscot will achieve the perfect period effect.

Wallpapers imitating the rich look of marble were often used, and this look can be achieved today via reproduction wallpapers or by creating a faux finish with paint. While some decorative effects are fairly easy to achieve (such as glazing or ragging), a faux marble finish is somewhat more difficult. Refer to books devoted to this subject and check with local schools and colleges, which frequently offer courses on the more complex techniques involved in creating painted decorative effects.

The naturalistic designs that were featured in wallpapers from the late 1870s through the turn of the century can be used today to create a library reminiscent of the late Victorian period. Subtle patterns being reproduced with the Victorian enthusiast in mind are available in vibrant colors (earthtones, green, dark blue, purple, red, gold), and are ideal in the library when used with a wood wainscot or an embossed paper such as Lincrusta. For a more subdued look, paint the walls in a warm shade and allow your carpet or area rugs to play host to pattern.

Color can be a strong influence in the contemporary home office. To recall Victorian style in a modern room where a great deal of your work is done, use a dark shade of red, which can be stimulating and often enhances creativity. Greens and blues, on the other hand, are generally restful or relaxing colors and are well suited to the library/home office used for reading and occasional work.

The home office can be quite modern, with gentle hints of Victoriana, or a more pronounced stance can be taken. The wall colors already discussed can help soften the hard lines of home computers and modern electronics, but by adding wooden wainscot, wallpaper, or impressive glass-front bookcases you can further minimize your high-tech equipment, creating a more traditional look. Visit any of the large architectural salvage emporiums and you'll be amazed at what you'll find: old architectural bookcases (originally built-ins) are not out of the ordinary and can easily be adapted for modern use.

FLOORING

The floor in the Victorian library was often carpeted, or a simple hardwood floor could be covered with a room-size area rug, or perhaps several area rugs. When carpeted, usually in a floral or geometric design, it was not unusual to find additional rugs (often hand-crafted needlepoints) layered upon the carpet to muffle sound and add to the cozy atmosphere. As Oriental motifs became popular during the late Victorian period, smaller rugs were strategically placed upon the room-sized rug to designate seating areas or to provide a warm, cushioned space for the children, who might be invited into the library to listen to their father read aloud. Deep, vivid shades of red, gold, green, or blue were common in the plush rugs that dressed the library's floor.

———

The floor treatment in this inviting library exposes the beauty of hardwood while defining a comfortable reading area with a tasteful Oriental rug. Detailed woodwork, treasured books, and personal mementos on display are the heart and soul of this serene Victorian-inspired retreat.

By 1900, critics were calling for painted or stained floors in the library with a simple matting that would not harbor dust. Large Oriental rugs, however, maintained their popularity well into the twentieth century.

Today's High Style Victorian library can be every bit as inviting as the library of a century ago. Using deep shades that exude warmth, in wall-to-wall carpeting of either a solid color or with a naturalistic design, creates an atmosphere of serenity. Area rugs can be added for a plush look, or a room-sized Oriental rug can be placed atop a hardwood floor. Choose your carpeting or area rug in lighter or darker shades of the color found on the walls, and the library will have a unified look that contributes to the air of calm.

The home office or den with Victorian overtones can be carpeted, or Oriental rugs can be used to define a cozy reading area or placed underneath a desk or worktable. Even the modern home office can be softened by introducing one beautiful area rug in an Oriental or needlepoint design.

CEILINGS

The majority of middle-class Victorian libraries did not include extensive decoration on the ceiling. As a room for quiet repose, the library was seldom subject to the ornate touches found in the parlor and dining room. Throughout the nineteenth century, ceilings in the library followed popular fashion and were painted in a lighter shade of a color on the walls. Decorative touches were found in crown molding around the perimeter of the ceiling, and this was frequently treated with gilt paint late in the nineteenth century. In the homes of the wealthy, the library ceiling may have been coffered, but this was the exception rather than the rule.

By the 1890s, the new fashion of wallpapering the ceiling and carrying the paper down the wall to a picture rail or molding was also being used in the library, albeit to a limited degree. As a room devoted to serious pursuits, the library tended to retain more traditional overtones throughout the nineteenth century.

The High Style Victorian library ceiling can be enhanced by painting it in a light shade. This is especially effective in a room with a low ceiling, where such a treatment tends to visually increase space. Adding a decorative molding or cornice brings a formal touch. Most home centers and lumber yards have these available in a wide array of sizes and designs.

The sterility of a home office can be tempered in the same way—soft, light-colored paint on the ceiling and a molding can be used to define the separation between walls and ceiling. A decorative molding or cornice has the added attraction of bringing architectural embellishment to a plain, modern space.

LIGHTING

During the early Victorian period the library was lit by candlelight and firelight, then by oil table or desk lamps in combination with candlelight. By the mid-century period dual-light, brass gasoliers, which shed more light, could be found in the libraries of many urban homes.

A kerosene student's lamp was available by the 1870s and was ideal for use at a desk, where its cantilever form allowed light to be cast directly atop paperwork or a book without the body of the lamp being in the way.

A kerosene hanging fixture referred to as a library lamp was used in many rural middle-class libraries. These lamps featured

a brass body with attractive, painted glass shades. (Similar examples embellished with prisms were often found in the parlor.)

Late-nineteenth-century homes able to take advantage of electric power may have had a combination fixture in the library, which could operate on either gas or electricity. This was a practical item since electric power in those days was sporadic at best.

Eventually art-glass electric table and desk lamps replaced kerosene lamps in the city but kerosene remained the main source of lighting in rural areas well into the 1920s

The Victorian Revival library can be lit with the traditional mix of hanging and table-top fixtures. Whether you choose to search for antiques, such as an old-fashioned library lamp, or reproductions, large hanging fixtures combined with a selection of table and desk lamps should adequately light the room as well as provide the localized illumination needed at work areas. Soft background lighting from a hanging fixture and a table lamp can brighten a cozy seating area, and accent lighting can be used to draw attention to a display of collectibles or a special piece of artwork. Remember that lighting is a significant factor in making the library a comfortable retreat. Choose fixtures that will give off different intensities of light to create a relaxing atmosphere.

The home office is generally smaller than a room devoted to a library, and calls for a

The work area in this formal library combines a desk lamp with candlelight for practicality and Victorian ambience. Warm-toned walls reflect a soft glow across the room.

careful selection of lighting fixtures to suit a specific purpose. To evoke Victorian spirit and style in even the most modern setting, a vintage or reproduction fixture, such as a student's lamp with a beautiful blue or green glass shade (restful colors the Victorians associated with leisurely pastimes), will recall nineteenth-century charm. Task lighting is imperative in the home office, and can be accomplished with an overhead fixture and/or desk or tabletop lighting. Refer to the source directory in the back of this book to help you locate dealers who specialize in antique or Victorian reproduction fixtures.

Shutters convey subtle masculinity and provide additional architectural interest in this eclectic Victorian library. Ideal for controlling light, they have been painted to match the cornice. A swag of rich red velvet at the top of the window softens the starkness of bare shutters, and picks up the color of the rug and throw pillows.

WINDOW TREATMENTS

The formality associated with a room devoted to intellectual pursuits and manly endeavors called for handsome window dressings without the feminine frills typically found in the parlor.

The early-Victorian-period library was likely to have windows dressed with a shade; a muslin "glass curtain" or undercurtain; a heavier drapery or curtain of damask, velvet, or brocade; and a valance. The outer curtain was generally of a rich, deep shade that contrasted with the color chosen for the walls. Painted venetian blinds paired with a decorative wooden valance were another popular window dressing during the early part of the nineteenth century.

During the later years, the library was subject to changing fashions, and with reformers calling for simplification throughout the home, window dressings were toned down. In the library during the 1870–1900 period, windows were liable to be dressed with shutters, either stained to match woodwork or painted to correspond to the color found on the walls. Shutters were often favored if the master of the house enjoyed a pipe or cigar, as curtain materials would absorb odors whereas the shutters would not. If curtains were used, the prevailing fashion called for a muslin or lace undercurtain of windowsill length and a rich, outer curtain with rings of wood or brass attached to a rod.

Today's library decorated in the Gothic Revival style calls for the formal window treatment described above. Trimmings such as tiebacks and a valance should display restraint. Venetian blinds or a Roman shade are simple, decorative alternatives to curtains.

The Victorian library that reflects the taste of the Eastlake Reform Movement can make use of shutters, simple lace panels with

a valance, or a more formal treatment using heavy drapes in a deep tone that matches wall coverings.

The home office, an area where ornamentation is kept to a minimum, can be outfitted with practical and appealing shutters or, for a softer look, with lace panels. Natural lighting is beneficial in a work environment and a heavy window dressing can hinder this. Depending upon your view and need for privacy, an attractive valance or swag may be all that's called for. Or pair them with shutters or lace panels (which filter light) on the bottom portion of your windows to provide more privacy.

FURNISHINGS

The typical Victorian library was furnished with a variety of pieces that conveyed both comfort and a diligent spirit. A desk or secretary (combination desk and bookcase) was a necessity in the library; often, both could be found there. The master's desk was often quite large and was either flat-topped with drawers, tablelike, or drop-front style. Later in the century, massive rolltop desks with a series of cubbyholes and a tambour door that could be pulled down to hide the work area became popular.

If bookcases were not built in, several tall, freestanding ones were used, and both desks and bookcases, as well as secretaries, were manufactured in the popular revival styles that predominated in the library throughout much of the nineteenth century.

A few armchairs, and perhaps a plush sofa with tapestry, velvet, or leather upholstery, provided comfortable seating for reading or relaxation, and side chairs were available should additional seating be required. Similar to the parlor arrangement,

Above: Large, comfortable furnishings were a mainstay of the Victorian library. Here, substantial armchairs accompany a flat-top desk with drawers for a decidedly baronial effect.

Left: Victorian sensibilities are awakened in this eclectic setting where a comfortable easy chair provides the perfect spot to retreat with a book and a polished desk serves to complete business at hand. Accessories such as pillows and fresh flowers are the key to a finished look.

furnishings were grouped to promote quiet, intimate conversation or were clustered together near the warmth of the fire, and a more formal arrangement around a center table was ideal for conducting business. A comfortable chair or two may have been placed near windows to take advantage of

Above: The timeless beauty of a fine piece of furniture creates instant impact in any room. This handsome secretary, filled with books and accompanied by a comfortable chair, defines a cozy space for desk work or reading.

Opposite: Accessories and collectibles are all-important when personalizing living space: here, crystal decanters, a collection of walking canes, and fine books shed light on the interests and tastes of the owner.

natural light, and the desk, of course, was given a prominent position in the room. A table, lamp stands, and scattered footstools completed the setting.

Throughout most of the nineteenth century, the library was furnished with large, masculine pieces in darkwood tones. By the

1880s Eastlake-style furnishings became popular, and golden oak (especially rolltop desks, but also bookcases and center tables) was appearing in the library.

Today's Victorian-inspired High Style library takes its cue from the past, and nineteenth century comfort and spirit can be created with vintage or reproduction furnishings that convey handsome elegance. Antique secretaries are not difficult to find, since many Victorian homes boasted more than one. Keep in mind when buying furniture that quality is paramount. Whether you're purchasing an antique or a reproduction, check carefully for sound construction. Examine joints, open and close desk drawers, and look closely at the finish.

The home office can easily be outfitted with pieces that reflect Victorian style. A large nineteenth-century table or desk can serve as your center of operation, and a bookcase or two can house not only books but office supplies as well. If you have space, a comfortable upholstered armchair for reading can add the perfect touch. The formality long associated with the library actually makes such nineteenth-century furniture timeless in its appeal and adaptable to even the most modern setting.

DECORATIVE ACCESSORIES AND COLLECTIBLES

The Victorian library was, quite simply, grand. Along with the various historical aspects that combined to create the attractive shell of the room and the furnishings that made it a comfortable and functional retreat, the library's sanctuarylike atmosphere was cultivated with a variety of accessories and mementos that reflected the taste of the man of the house.

"Books are windows through which the soul looks out.... Few comprehend the possibilities of the outlook through books. We view the people and places of distant lands. The nations of the past spring into existence as by magic and move before us as a panorama. We view the inner workings of men's lives, we look down into the earth, out upon the operations of nature in plant and animal life, and up into the starry heavens, actually touching the far off spheres."

Richard A. Wells, A.M.
Manners, Culture and Dress of the
Best American Society, *1891*

In typical Victorian fashion, fringed scarves were draped across tabletops, crystal decanters held the choicest liquors and wines, and the master's pipe and humidor box or jar for tobacco were often found atop his desk along with papers and writing

The beauty of time-worn books creates an eye-catching display in this Victorian-inspired library. Classics mix with contemporary volumes to fill the shelves to the point of overflow, and accessories such as the stately bust and vintage photos are a reminder of days gone by.

paraphernalia. A decorative clock kept time on a shelf or was hung on a wall, and the artwork displayed often mirrored an interest in hunting, fishing, or the outdoors in general. Most importantly, the library contained the family's treasured collection of books. As truly cherished objects, books were revered not only for the windows of the world they opened, but also because of the status achieved by having a well-stocked library in one's home.

Nineteenth-century books are coveted by many collectors and Victorian enthusiasts today for their investment potential, their historical significance, their stunning good looks (many with beautiful leather bindings embossed with gold trim), and because they often provide a firsthand look at Victorian daily life. Instructional books such as the etiquette manuals that targeted the growing middle class after the 1860s are a treasure trove of information on the do's and don'ts of polite society, and the home manuals that were geared toward young brides display the inner workings of the Victorian household.

Popular fiction, as well as the works of noted authors such as James Fenimore Cooper, Charles Dickens, Nathaniel Hawthorne, Washington Irving, Henry Wadsworth Longfellow, George Bernard Shaw, Leo Tolstoy, and Oscar Wilde could be found in the typical Victorian library and are often rare collector's items today. Not so with all vintage printed material—many Victorian-era books and periodicals can be had for a song. They make a wonderful addition to today's library and afford countless hours of pleasurable reading.

The History of the Sitting Room

Throughout much of the Victorian era, as middle-class homes grew larger, it was customary to reserve the drawing room or parlor for receiving guests and entertaining. As a result, the sitting room became a special private area devoted to intimate family evenings, leisurely activities, and industrious crafts or handiwork.

"The sitting room or every-day room should be the brightest and the most attractive room in the house. Its beauty should lie in its comfort, simplicity and the harmony of its tints—the main feature being the fitness of each article to the needs of the room. In these days of so many advantages much can be done in adornment by simple means."

Richard A. Wells, A.M.
Manners, Culture and Dress of the
Best American Society, *1891*

The sitting room was found either on the first floor of the Victorian home, behind the more public rooms, or occasionally on the second floor along with the chambers, or bedrooms.

As a personal space given over to relaxation, craftwork, or popular games, the sitting room's furnishings were in keeping with the informal decor. Light colors on the walls gave it an airy and cheerful look, and window treatments were planned with convenience and simplicity in mind. If the house did not include a library, the family's collection of books could be found in the sitting room, and as only the wealthy could afford a separate music room, the family piano or organ was usually located in the sitting room as well.

Although the family spent a great deal of time together in this relaxed setting, it was generally considered "her" domain and was decorated in distinctly feminine fashion. Adorned with select mementos, family photographs, and decorative art, the spirit of the sitting room was captured in the sentimental needlework mottoes that graced the walls, proclaiming "Home Sweet Home" or "God Bless Our Home."

By the turn of the century, the obvious distinction between rooms and their specialized function was fading away. In many homes, especially the smaller bungalow styles, the parlor and sitting room became one—and the living room served the dual purpose of providing an area for family activity as well as entertaining guests.

Creating a Victorian Sitting Room

Homes built in the nineteenth century often include a designated sitting room. For many of us, however, the modern interpretation of this space is commonly called the family room or simply the living room. Creating Victorian grandeur in a space devoted to family can be tastefully done by following the Victorian lead. Consider the background of the room—the walls, flooring, ceiling, and windows—and follow through in typical Victorian fashion to complete the setting with lamps, furnishings, and those special objects near and dear to your heart.

WALL TREATMENTS

As the brightest room in the house, the early Victorian sitting room was painted or papered in shades of rose, blue, or light gray. As wallpaper became more affordable and available throughout the mid-century period, the sitting room was often papered in a cheerful, gay design.

Light colors continued to be preferred as the century progressed, and late Victorian–era choices expanded to include cream, fawn, or a very pale olive green. These colors were used in wall coverings that displayed subtle designs of contrasting hues. Unlike the library, with deep tones that

Feminine fashion reigns freely in this Victorian sitting room. Light, cheerful shades of color in the wallpaper and matching fabric create a pleasant oasis for escape and relaxation. Wall-to-wall carpet adds warmth and plush softness underfoot.

"The old custom of setting apart a 'best room' or parlor to be used only on special occasions...is happily passing away....The present tendency is to call all of the lower rooms of the house 'living rooms,' and to have all the members of the family use them freely....A hostess who takes her friends into a sitting room and tells them frankly that she prefers to 'live in her own parlor' will have more friends than critics. The arrangement is plainly for the good of the family, and all who visit such a home will be the better for having been taken into the wholesome family life."

Sidney Morse
Household Discoveries, *1908*

encouraged quiet study or repose, the sitting room was to be a spirited, sunny room, promoting family interaction and providing an uplifting space in which to play games, do a bit of needlework, or enjoy music.

If we fast-forward to the present, the Victorian Revival sitting room can draw upon these same colors—rose, gray, fawn, cream, light blue, or pale olive—to create a homey family retreat. Often, simply painting the room in one of these shades will achieve a Victorian effect once combined with vintage furnishings and a beautiful rug or carpet. For greater depth and focus, wallpaper can serve to unite a room that contains a potpourri of furniture and accessories. A soft floral or foliage pattern with two shades of a light color is ideal.

Today's highly functional family room, with its entertainment center, VCR tapes, and compact discs, can be made more cozy by employing soft or light colors in the wall treatment. For example, pale rose walls will temper the modern look of state-of-the-art electronics and convey the subtle romanticism reminiscent of the Victorian era.

FLOORING

As a center of family activity, comfort and practicality were paramount in the Victorian sitting room. Floors were covered with convenience in mind. If the floor was a soft wood (usually pine), it was painted and then carpeted or covered with a room-sized area rug. A hardwood floor was treated the same way—covered with an attractive carpet or a series of area rugs that could easily be removed to be cleaned. Tapestry rugs in colors such as pale canary or light gray with floral designs and attractive borders were highly favored for the sitting room; the term

Above: Whether atop carpeting or a hardwood floor, layering area rugs for solid comfort not only provides a plush touch but muffles noise as well. You simply cannot have too many rugs when recreating Victorian style.

Opposite: The Victorian sitting room was often treated to an attractive wall-to-wall carpet with a geometric or floral design. As in the parlor, seating was often arranged in small groupings to accommodate various activities.

"tapestry rug" referred to a velvet Wilton or a tapestry Brussels. Distinctions were made according to the technique employed in creating the rug—a cut pile was featured on a velvet Wilton while a level-loop pile denoted a tapestry Brussels. A tapestry carpet was less costly than the floor coverings reserved for the parlor or dining room.

Another popular floor covering in the sitting room was an ingrain, or flat-pile, carpet, and these were relatively inexpensive and long-wearing. Ingrain carpets, unlike the tapestry carpets mentioned above, were reversible and therefore considered a wise investment for a room subject to hard use. Ingrain carpets were also available in a variety of patterns that incorporated two or more colors. Abstract patterns (geometric, floral, and foliage) remained popular through the turn of the century, and while an Oriental rug may have occasionally been used here, it was more likely found in the parlor or dining room where fashion dictates were closely observed.

Today's Victorian-inspired sitting room can be beautiful with the addition of a carefully selected wall-to-wall carpet featuring an eye-catching border. Carpet with an overall design can set a cheerful tone for the sitting room, but be careful to coordinate upholstery for a subtle blend of patterns and colors. Large rugs are ideal in place of carpeting, especially if you don't own your home, and smaller rugs can be layered for a plush effect.

In today's family room, location, traffic flow, and wear and tear on the room should all be taken into consideration when choosing a floor treatment. Level-loop-pile carpeting (which features uncut loops of consistent height) or cut-pile carpeting commonly called a "frieze" (a dense pile with a nubby look) are available in patterns or solid colors and are ideal for the room that receives a lot of use.

For a different twist, a family room with a country flavor can evoke a hint of Victoriana with a floral-patterned hooked or needlepoint rug, or even a rag rug or two, in soft, pastel shades.

In juxtaposing two distinct styles, this family room takes its inspiration from the Victorians. The wallpapered ceiling and parquet floor covered by an area rug offer Victorian treatments with a more contemporary look. Note, too, that the elegance of Victorian sidechairs is tempered by bold country cushions.

CEILINGS

With the exception of homes belonging to the extremely wealthy, the Victorian sitting room, designed to be restful and breezy, was rarely embellished with ceiling adornments. This expanse was usually painted in a light color and a tasteful cornice defined the separation between walls and ceiling. By the late nineteenth century, popular practice regarding wallpaper no doubt found many a sitting room with a papered ceiling corresponding to papered walls, but this was more likely the exception than the rule.

The Victorian practice of painting the ceiling can be adopted for modern use, and both the High Style sitting room and the contemporary family room can be enhanced by applying color to the ceiling. If old habits die hard and you feel more comfortable with a white ceiling, consider a delicate variation of white such as eggshell, which can have a softening effect and still complement a subtle, pastel shade on the walls.

For something a bit different in the family room with country spirit, wood beams add a touch of rusticity long associated with Victorian-era retreats such as the camps in the Adirondack Mountains.

LIGHTING

As in the other rooms of the Victorian home, the sitting room was illuminated by a combination of lamps. A hanging fixture might have been used, and a variety of wall sconces and tabletop lamps were common. Such lamps were highly functional and therefore less decorative than examples put to use in the parlor. Kerosene lamps with glass or

There is no doubt that Victorian panache inspired this feminine retreat. The stunning, floral-shaded lamp on the desk and the ornate chandelier are as stylish today as they were a century ago.

handcrafted fabric shades, and later electric lamps, were placed in cozy corners for reading, on tabletops near work areas, and on the center table or game table where the family might gather for conversation and amusement in the evenings.

Today's Victorian sitting room can best be lit in the same way—by using a combination of fixtures. A hanging light, such as an

walls and the carpet. Such curtains were usually looped back with pretty ribbons.

Windows in today's Victorian sitting room should be dressed with lightweight curtains that will filter natural light. A softly colored and patterned chintz can be used to match upholstery, or sheers with a dotted Swiss design can add a delicate touch. Translucent fabric shades or even rice paper shades can work well in the sitting room where a only minimal window treatment is desired.

Contemporary mini-blinds, available in a wide array of colors, can be ideal in a modern family room and can be "dressed" with a romantic valance of chintz or lace for a more Victorian look. Matchstick shades work well in any setting and add an exotic touch to the decor, recalling the Victorians' late-nineteenth-century obsession with Oriental motifs and accessories.

———

Left: Coordinated floral chintz fabric on the curtains and divan provide the perfect Victorian touch in this comfy corner. Like the sitting rooms of days gone by, a light and airy feeling pervades the space.

Opposite: The perfect spot for a relaxing moment with a cup of tea, this corner combines several distinct elements of Victorian style. Note that the furnishings, including the beautifully upholstered divan and the small whatnot in the corner, are ideally suited to the casual atmosphere of the setting.

attractive drop fixture with a frosted or etched-glass globe, would be in keeping with the informal atmosphere of the sitting room and, combined with carefully placed sconces, would provide adequate general lighting. Reproduction or antique table lamps are needed for more direct task lighting. Choose fixtures with nineteenth-century style — kerosene lamps can be wired for electricity, a student's lamp can be placed on a secretary or desk, and a pole lamp with an art-glass shade can prove ideal next to a reading chair.

The contemporary family room can be made comfortably Victorian with the fixtures mentioned but avoid fabric shades in a sleek, modern setting, where they tend to look a bit too fussy.

WINDOW TREATMENTS

Victorian sitting room windows were usually dressed with a simple shade or with curtains made of cheesecloth, chintz, or dotted Swiss in light shades that would complement the

FURNISHINGS

Victorian sitting rooms were typically furnished with a mixture of pieces, including older chairs, tables, and so on, that may have been in the parlor at one time. During the late nineteenth century many household experts recommended that such older furnishings, especially parlor sets, be covered with various chintz patterns, which would break up the monotony of the set and add a pleasant variety to the room. In addition, a low divan (a couch or sofa without armrests or a back) accented with numerous pillows, an upholstered or perhaps a wicker rocker, a large easy chair or two, an attractive bamboo chair, and a Turkish chair (an overstuffed, tufted chair in an exotic fabric) would provide adequate and comfortable seating.

A center table or large table of some sort (draped with an attractive scarf, of course) was placed centrally to serve as a catchall. If the house was without a library, the sitting room also included a bookcase with either glass doors or a brass rod and an attractive curtain (the curtain could be drawn to protect the books from light and dust). If the family enjoyed games, a wooden card table was often found in the sitting room, and of course, the lady of the house had a small worktable or sewing stand for her knitting or other needlecraft.

Today's Victorian sitting room can be outfitted with the same eclectic mixture of furnishings that was popular in this setting one hundred years ago. Cast-off parlor sets or individual pieces can be upholstered in cretonne (a heavyweight, printed cotton fabric that's somewhat sturdier than chintz), and chintz can be used on those chairs that receive only occasional use. A combination of armchairs, a sofa, or a Victorian divan make up the basics from which you can choose depending upon your needs and personal taste. Wicker adds a light and airy touch, and a plush chair dressed in an exotic design or pattern (with a touch of fringe) can pay tribute to the Victorian fascination with the Far East.

While reproduction furnishings are fine, don't overlook family heirlooms. And consider the pleasure that can be derived from hunting antiques shows and auctions in search of vintage pieces that blend nicely in the mix-and-match approach. In pulling it all together, cluster furnishings in several areas around the room just as the Victorians would have done.

The multipurpose family room can be functional and clearly convey Victorian style

Family photographs, cherished collectibles, and treasured keepsakes provide visual texture, a sense of comfort, and a delightful decorative touch in any space, but are especially appropriate in your own private corner of the world.

at the same time. While it's not a good idea to alter antique furniture to accommodate modern needs, a small television can be stored in a vintage secretary or cupboard, and nineteenth-century wicker and golden oak tables and chairs can happily coexist with a contemporary sofa.

Storage space can often be a problem in the family room, where clutter tends to pile up. Toys, magazines, or newspapers can be kept handy but hidden from view in an old trunk, which can also serve as a coffee table. A large step-back cupboard can be used to store a stereo system—the possibilities are nearly endless.

DECORATIVE ACCESSORIES AND COLLECTIBLES

As a special place to where the Victorian family could retreat to pass the time, the sitting room naturally overflowed with accessories and personal, decorative items.

Treasured souvenirs, pieces of odd china, collections of seashells, sentimental vases, family photos, and handcrafted artwork filled every nook and cranny. No tabletop was left bare, and the mantelpiece, as well as the top of the bookcase, was crowded with cherished items.

Windows in the sitting room often served as an indoor garden, with a profuse display of greenery. This homey touch could be carried one step further by the mistress with a green thumb, who might train ivy to grow up the wall, encircle a watercolor or a pastel, and continue on toward the ceiling—with the plant eventually flowing about the entire perimeter of the room.

Games could be found stacked next to a game table, sheet music filled a stand near the piano or organ, and popular magazines such as *Godey's Lady's Book* were stored in a magazine rack.

Artistic endeavors resulted in wall-hung examples of hairwork design (detailed artwork created from human hair), needlework samplers or sayings, and attractive scrap albums filled with pressed flowers. During the 1890s "pyrography," or burnt-wood crafts, became popular, and kits could be purchased with everything needed to create attractive wall-hung plaques, decorative boxes, and even small stands embellished with a burnt-wood design.

If the sitting room also served as the lady's sewing area, her worktable or basket was filled with now-precious collectibles, such as buttons and clasps, and a variety of implements including scissors, darners, thimbles, and so on.

While the treasures found in the sitting room were objects of the Victorians' pleasures and pastimes, they are collectibles to us today. Perhaps none is so touching as the examples of handiwork that serve as proof that someone long ago labored to create something special—something we now cherish as much as they once did.

The sitting room or family room is the perfect spot for your personal mementos and collections. Do exactly as the Victorians did and surround yourself with those items that fill your time and give you comfort.

—◦◦◦—

Combining European country charm with a goodly dose of Victoriana, this sitting room is made all the more attractive by the addition of a stunning secretary filled with select pieces of china, books, and exotic figurines.

The Victorian Kitchen

The Victorian kitchen had the dubious distinction of being a utilitarian service area that was oftentimes the domain of domestic servants. Cooking; laundry work; putting up preserves; making soap, candles, and cleaning supplies—these were but a few of the overwhelming tasks assigned to those who labored in the kitchen.

As a factorylike (and later, laboratorylike) center of household operations, the Victorian kitchen rarely reflected the attention to detail lavished on the other rooms of the house. Rather, the nineteenth-century kitchen developed a subtle charm all its own as the Gilded Age progressed—a look we find especially appealing in bringing Victoriana into the present day.

Down the center hall to the butler's pantry at the rear of the house…step into the kitchen as we explore the curiosities associated with its history, taking special note of the abundance of ideas for creating your own interpretation of the Victorian kitchen.

Victorian spirit presides over this modern kitchen. By incorporating nineteenth-century design elements, such as the tile wall behind the cooktop and a vintage lighting fixture, with decorative accessories like copper pans, brass candlesticks, and wall-hung prints, a charming, old-fashioned look permeates an efficient work space.

The History of the Victorian Kitchen

Many kitchens of the early Victorian period still displayed Colonial overtones in massive fireplaces or cooking hearths. By the 1850s, however, most cooks and housekeepers were becoming accustomed to their new wood- or coal-burning cast-iron stoves or ranges.

The rural kitchen and its urban counterpart were a study in contrasts. The rural or country kitchen throughout the nineteenth century was a homey room where the mistress and her daughters labored (with assistance from hired help in larger households), and it was quite common for the family to eat meals here by the warmth of the stove. The urban kitchen, on the other hand, was given over to a string of domestics (the cook, maids, a butler), as family life in town revolved around the parlor, dining room, library, and sitting room.

Early on, kitchens were located in a wing of the house, in the basement, or, especially in southern states, in a separate building nearby. It was imperative that the heat and cooking odors associated with the kitchen not be allowed to permeate the parlor and dining room, and thus offend visitors. Along with the kitchen proper, the kitchen area included a pantry for storing foodstuffs and cookware, as well as a scullery or laundry area where food was prepared and the family's weekly wash was tended to.

Not until Catharine Beecher and Harriet Beecher Stowe's landmark book, *The American Woman's Home,* was published in 1869 did the kitchen receive much attention. The sisters proposed a kitchen plan that was a model of efficiency, with built-in work areas and storage bins—a revolutionary concept in an age of freestanding kitchen cupboards and haphazard kitchen floor plans. A pioneer of nineteenth-century studies regarding domestic science, Catharine Beecher campaigned for step-saving measures in the kitchen and educating young women in matters of housekeeping.

By the 1870s, with the introduction of gas lines and indoor plumbing in cities and towns, kitchens were routinely moved up from the basement to the first floor, at the rear of the house. At the same time, well-trained domestic servants were in short supply as many opted to work in the factories that had sprung up as a result of the Industrial Revolution. The mistress of the middle-class home was left little choice but to return to her kitchen, and while she may have previously enjoyed a supervisory position (overseeing the household staff, consulting with the cook regarding menus, and so on), during the 1880s and 1890s she assumed a hands-on role. With good domestic help becoming scarce, many households could no longer afford to pay their rising salaries. Others, discouraged by the constant stream of immigrant girls that came and went in their employment, chose to forgo this nuisance and reduced their household staff. In the last decades before the turn of the century, it was not unusual for madame to share household duties with one servant girl and hire additional help as needed for dinner parties, spring cleaning, or laundry work.

As the lady of the Victorian house became more active in the kitchen, industry responded with myriad patented gadgets and utensils to help her do everything from stone cherries and pare apples to slice beans and juice lemons. The availability of packaged and canned goods during the last quarter of

"*If parents wish their daughters to grow up with good domestic habits, they should have…a neat and cheerful kitchen. A kitchen should always, if possible, be entirely above-ground, so that all the premises may be swept sweet and clean. If flowers and shrubs be cultivated around the doors and windows, and the yard near them be kept well turfed, it will add very much to their agreeable appearance. The walls should often be cleaned and white-washed, to promote a neat look and pure air. The floor of a kitchen should be painted or covered with an oilcloth.*"

Catharine E. Beecher & Harriet Beecher Stowe
The American Woman's Home,
1869

the century transformed the kitchen from a factorylike center of operations, where everything was made from scratch, into a tribute to the new spirit of consumerism. Suddenly, decorative, chromolithographed tins of tea, coffee, and spices lined the shelves in the pantry. Packaged breakfast cereals and canned meats and vegetables brought convenience and time-saving measures to the late-Victorian-era kitchen. These mass-produced products and new kitchenware prompted a flood of cookbooks and household manuals designed to assist the housekeeper in new cookery methods, cleaning, and so on (commonly called the "science of housewifery"), and increasing attention was devoted to the appearance—dare we say decoration—of the kitchen area.

During the 1880s and early 1890s, wooden wainscoting was a popular wall treatment in the middle-class Victorian kitchen and the introduction of linoleum brought modest patterns or design work to a previously drab environment. Decorative touches such as a chintz or muslin window curtains, green plants, and vivid, artistic, enamelware cooking implements added charm and a welcome dose of color. The rich patina of a well-worn pine table and numerous dressers or step-back cupboards conveyed a sense of warmth. The butler's pantry was often outfitted with attractive glass-front cabinetry that housed the china and glassware reserved for the dining room.

With the mounting concern over the spread of disease during the late 1890s and early 1900s, the kitchen became a sanitary environment, with a clinical, almost laboratorylike appearance. Crisp white tiles, which wouldn't hide dirt and germs, replaced a wooden wainscot, or walls were painted with an easy-to-wash enamel. Tile was also used

on floors, as was brick or linoleum. A white porcelain enamel sink was fixed to the wall, and plumbing and pipes were frequently exposed in an effort to fight the war on germs. This sanitary kitchen predominated through the turn of the century and into the

---

This Victorian country kitchen clearly recalls the past via the handsome and practical tile flooring, custom-crafted cabinetry reminiscent of vintage cupboards, and deep-colored walls. Carefully selected kitchen goods such as the copper cookware, yellowware bowls, wooden utensils, and antique food scales contribute an authentic touch.

1920s, when color made its debut in appliances and utensils, and gas or electric stoves did away with the grime long associated with coal- and wood-burning ranges.

Creating a Victorian Kitchen

Unlike the other rooms in the Victorian home, where an authentic recreation of nineteenth-century wall treatments, flooring, furnishings, and accessories are sought after by devoted Victoriana enthusiasts, the kitchen calls for a flexible interpretation of Victorian style—a blending of the best of the past into a highly functional, modern room. Consider for a moment what it would be like

to work in the typical Victorian kitchen—cooking on the temperamental cast-iron stove, polishing it, feeding it fuel...being ever-watchful for overflow of the drip pan underneath the oak icebox...concocting the arsenal of cleaning solutions used throughout the home...walking miles in the kitchen during the course of the day—we'd no sooner

> *"In housekeeping as in everything else, system is of the utmost importance.... Not only should there be a place for everything, and everything put in its place, the importance of which is often insisted on, though none too often, but there should also be a time for everything. Have certain days of the week for doing certain things, and also arrange the work of the day, as far as possible, alloting a time for every duty."*
>
> Smiley's Cook Book and
> New and Complete Guide for
> Housekeepers, *1898*

forsake our modern conveniences than the Victorians would have relinquished theirs.

How then do we create a Victorian kitchen? Quite simply, by evoking Victorian style. We call upon nineteenth-century designs, materials, and furnishings to create an atmosphere rather than a literal rendition. For example, a High Style Victorian kitchen will conjure up images of darkwood cabinets with glass-front doors, rich marble work surfaces, and bright tile floors, but alongside the Victorian table and dressers will stand the refrigerator and the dishwasher, the microwave and the food processor—all the high-tech appliances the Victorians would have coveted.

A country Victorian kitchen calls to mind the scrubbed top of a pine table, spacious cupboards filled with an overflow of dishware, wooden floors, and cheerful, painted

The appearance of this contemporary kitchen is softened and given a more formal look by incorporating Victorian-inspired glass-front cabinetry. Note also the tile backsplash behind the countertop.

walls. Even the modern or eclectic kitchen can convey the spirit of Victoriana with well-chosen furnishings such as an oak table and chairs or an old Hoosier cupboard. In any kitchen a nineteenth-century color palette or simple vintage collectibles can recall the past, creating a harmonious blend of Victorian style with modern appliances and twentieth-century efficiency.

WALL TREATMENTS

Early-Victorian-period walls were conservatively painted in neutral shades such as tan or cream, and woodwork was painted in a deeper shade of the same color or grained in imitation of more costly hardwoods such as oak or cherry.

During the 1860s domestic science authority Catharine Beecher suggested that kitchen walls be whitewashed (a practice that continued in many homes until the late

Wooden wainscoting became a popular wall treatment in the kitchen during the late Victorian era. This design element works especially well today in evoking Victorian spirit, and walls above the wainscot can be painted or papered to suit your color scheme.

nineteenth century), but other household experts disagreed, voicing concern that such walls grew dull and drab, often requiring semiannual painting.

By the late Victorian era, the muted colors and earth tones associated with the Aesthetic Movement had influenced wall treatments in the kitchen to a limited degree, and popular paint colors included tan and light shades of green, gold, and yellow. In addition, the tripartite horizontal division of

wall space that proved so popular during the late 1870s and 1880s in the parlor and dining room (where a wainscot or dado, field, and frieze were featured with wood, wallpaper, or paint) was loosely interpreted in the kitchen. A wooden or beadboard wainscot was applied to the lower portion of the kitchen walls, with the top section painted and sometimes further accessorized with a functional and decorative plate rail around the perimeter of the room.

Before the turn of the century, the emphasis on sanitation in the kitchen cast an unfavorable light on the use of wainscoting, and popular practice reverted to simple, enamel-paint finishes or, in the homes of the well-to-do, a tile dado instead of wooden wainscoting. While many middle-class Victorian kitchens continued to be painted in light, muted shades, white was also in vogue and was associated with cleanliness.

Wallpaper was rarely used in the Victorian kitchen unless it was a sanitary paper coated with varnish. Not until the 1930s did wallpaper become well received in dressing kitchen walls, due to the perceived threat of germs that might be harbored on the paper.

Today's Victorian-inspired kitchen has numerous possibilities when it comes to wall treatments. In its most basic form, subtle nineteenth-century spirit can be recalled with the color palette. Painting the kitchen in a soft shade, such as light green, and dressing the room with an attractive wallpaper border can work in tandem with other historical aspects of the room—such as warm wooden flooring. Other colors associated with the Victorian era can be put to use in the kitchen as well. Pale rose or soft blue can be equally fitting in the kitchen where the spirit of the style is the desired effect.

> *"Kitchens are more appropriately papered in varnished staircase paper, as the soils can be easily washed off. In many houses kitchens are wood-panelled, or the walls covered with tiles, after the good old fashion common in Germany and Holland."*
>
> *Alexander V. Hamilton*
> The Household
> Cyclopaedia of Practical Receipts
> and Daily Wants, *1873*

A formal High Style kitchen is the perfect setting for tile, whether used as a dado or carefully placed on walls to serve as a backsplash around counters and stoves.

A wooden wainscot immediately calls to mind Victorian style and can be used in a country kitchen, a more traditional setting, or an eclectic kitchen. Left natural, wood tones create warmth, or wainscoting can be painted for a more dramatic effect.

One of the most popular means of drawing the past into the present-day kitchen is by using wallpaper with nineteenth-century patterns or designs. While the parlor or sitting room was the heart of the home during the Victorian era, the kitchen often claims

this place of honor in today's fast-paced world. Our kitchens are frequently extended living areas with adjoining family rooms or sitting areas, and cooking is often done while visiting with family or guests. Since the kitchen is so much more than simply a food preparation area, wallpaper can be an ideal way of giving the room a more furnished look. Keep in mind that small patterns tend to work well in small spaces and large patterns are well suited to a spacious kitchen. The more formal kitchen, reminiscent of the butler's pantry with rich woods, glass-front cabinets, and marble or granite countertops, can be quite handsome with a striped wallpaper, a colored paper with a wood-grain effect, or an embossed Lincrusta paper, which can be painted in any shade.

A modern, eclectic, or country kitchen can be enhanced with a mini-print, or depending upon the size of the room, a large floral, ivy, or fruit-design paper reproduced with vintage patterns. Florals and ivy designs are especially at home in a romance-inspired cottage kitchen.

The kitchen filled with oak cabinetry and antique or reproduction oak furnishings can be striking when treated with a wallpaper featuring the muted shades and stylized naturalistic patterns made popular by the late-nineteenth-century Eastlake and Arts and Crafts movements.

To determine the type of wallpaper best suited to your kitchen, consider traffic areas, the amount of cooking you do, and whether a child's fingerprints are something to contend with. Many of the machine-manufactured wallpapers available today are scrubbable and can be used successfully in the kitchen; there are also heavy-duty papers produced with the kitchen and bathroom in mind. If easy care and durability are important requirements, consider a fabric-backed vinyl or solid vinyl wall covering. While both are available pre-pasted and scrubbable, a fabric-backed vinyl is also resistant to stains and fading.

FLOORING

The middle-class Victorian kitchen floor during the early 1800s was usually a soft pine, painted to protect the wood and make it easier to maintain. Gray, dark green or red, and a deep mustard yellow were common colors found on wood flooring. The wealthy Victorian homeowner, on the other hand, often made use of brick rather than wide pine boards in laying a kitchen floor.

Oilcloths were frequently used atop wood floors (old wood floors were not always perfectly even or in the best condition) and could be purchased by the mid 1800s or made at home. A heavyweight cloth was stretched, coated with paste, given several coats of paint, and lastly varnished. Such oilcloths could last for many years in the kitchen.

By the late Victorian period, tile was favored among the upper class as it was sturdy and easy to clean. It was also costly, and as a result many kitchen floors continued to

High Style Victorian influence is displayed in this dramatic parquet floor. Accompanied by dark wood cabinetry and sumptuous trim, this kitchen hints at the formality associated with the upscale urban kitchen or butler's pantry of a century ago.

be made of wood, which was now varnished (painting the floor fell out of fashion by the 1870s) or covered by linoleum. A wonderful new option in flooring, linoleum was invented in England during the 1860s and was available in America by the late 1870s. The Victorians adored anything new, and linoleum, created from linseed oil, fillers, and ground cork applied to a burlap backing, was durable and quite affordable. Linoleum even imitated more expensive geometric-patterned tile in its design, thus creating the look without the cost.

Today's kitchen, regardless of the predominant style, can recall nineteenth-century charm with the warmth and good looks of a hardwood floor. Oak, maple, birch, and pecan are the favorites and are available in wide planks or narrow, strip form. Once laid, your wood floor should be stained and treated with a protective polyurethane finish or coated with a penetrating sealer and several coats of wax.

Parquet squares are also available and easy to install, but are best suited to either a High Style or modern kitchen. Parquet would be a bit too dressy in a country kitchen and its intricate pattern may be distracting in the eclectic setting.

In refurbishing today's Victorian-style kitchen, tile continues to maintain its reputation for being long-lasting and beautiful, adding a touch of elegance to this highly functional room. In the kitchen of the late 1800s, where convenience was referred to as "economy and system," tile was appreciated for the same reasons it is valued today: its versatility and easy care. Ceramic tile is available in easy-to-install sheets composed of one-inch (2.5cm) squares or in larger quarry tiles of various shapes. Colors are almost limitless and tiles are manufactured with glazed or unglazed finishes. Glazed tiles feature a high-gloss or low-luster finish and are stain and water resistant. Unglazed tiles have a slight texture, which prevents the floor from becoming slippery when wet, and they too are usually stain resistant.

With the wide assortment of colors, shapes, designs, and sizes available in tile today, it's easy to customize a decorative floor that conveys your own personal interpretation of Victoriana. For example, in a High Style kitchen, small square or hexagonal tiles can create a stunning geometric or mosaic pattern.

Linoleum has been replaced by modern vinyl flooring, and this option offers decorative possibilities as numerous and as varied as tile. Resilient vinyl flooring is available in rolls of various widths or in twelve-by-twelve-inch (30.4cm) tiles. There are different grades of vinyl flooring, such as inlaid vinyls, which feature color or pattern clear through to the backing, and printed vinyls, which have color or design work on the surface only. Inlaid vinyl is of course more long-lived, since the pattern remains clear as the surface wears.

"The kitchen, as the workshop of the house, is the room in which many housekeepers spend most of their waking hours. Hence it should be perhaps the lightest, airiest and most cheerful room in the house.…Try to make the kitchen a room in harmonizing tints by painting or tinting the walls in light greens and the floor in dark green. Or a clear, light yellow is a good color for the kitchen walls, with the floor in brown. Or, if the room has a southern or western exposure, gray walls, with the floor in drab or slate color, will give a cooler effect.…A smooth floor of unpainted wood, hard enough not to splinter and to admit of being scrubbed, is perhaps the best floor for a kitchen…or the floor may be covered with linoleum, which is perhaps, all things considered, the most satisfactory floor covering."

Sidney Morse
Household Discoveries, *1908*

Available with low-wax or no-wax finishes, vinyl is a low-maintenance flooring that can retain its good looks for years. As with tile, color and design choices are almost limitless, and vinyl can be used to achieve the look of wood or tile. It's ideal in even the most traditional Victorian kitchen and can be creatively used to include borders, center "rugs," and so on.

CEILINGS

As a utilitarian work space devoted to tedious and mundane nineteenth-century tasks, the kitchen was merely functional and only rarely embellished. Early Victorian kitchens featured painted or whitewashed ceilings. Later in the century the ceiling was painted with an enamel that could easily be washed, and while the other rooms in the house were treated to tinted ceilings, white was considered most practical in the kitchen.

A popular alternative to painting was installing a pressed-tin ceiling in the kitchen, which was not only considered sanitary but was also highly favored in a room exposed to moisture, heat, and smoke. Initially created in imitation of costly plasterwork, tin ceilings added a decorative touch in this otherwise austere room.

Today's Victorian kitchen is perfectly at home with a white or an off-white ceiling, which will help reflect light in a small room or an area with few windows. A white ceiling fits beautifully into any color scheme and adds a crisp, clean look to the kitchen. If your ceiling is very low, however, you may want to consider using a light shade of the color on your walls to visually raise your ceiling.

To evoke more obvious Victorian flair, especially in a High Style kitchen with richly gleaming wood, tile, brass hardware or

A wonderful example of Victoriana at its best, this kitchen combines several vintage design elements. Glass-front cabinets, tiled floor and countertops, and old-fashioned accessories give the look of yesteryear, yet are still practical in today's kitchens. The crowning glory—a pressed tin ceiling and cornice—add a distinctive nineteenth-century touch.

accents, and copper cookware, a pressed-tin ceiling and corresponding molding or cornice is the perfect touch. Several manufacturers specialize in Victorian tin ceilings today (refer to the source directory) and offer a variety of designs in nail-up or lay-in sheets that are usually two by four feet (0.6 by 1.2m) or two by eight feet (0.6 by 2.4m) in size. Tin ceilings are available with a bold, brass finish or in unfinished sheets, which can be painted in the color of your choice. Some Victoriana enthusiasts find pressed-tin panels are adaptable for walls, where they create an eye-catching dado effect.

LIGHTING

Light sources in the Victorian kitchen progressed from firelight and candlelight to oil lamps, and then to gas and electric hanging fixtures and wall lamps. Functional and unadorned, a single-light fixture was often hung from the center of the ceiling or over a

worktable. Wall lamps provided additional, limited lighting in the kitchen. Such arrangements were often less than ideal, since the hanging fixture was often relied on to light a large expanse (many Victorian kitchens were quite spacious).

Today's Victorian kitchen with planned floor space and established work triangles is the perfect setting for vintage or reproduction fixtures, which help soften the look of modern appliances and clearly convey nineteenth-century spirit. You can happily forgo track lighting in favor of more subtle fixtures that are every bit as functional. Depending upon the size and shape of your kitchen (square, galleylike, or rectangular), one or possibly two hanging drop fixtures or ceiling fixtures with frosted, white, or colored glass shades are the perfect place to start in planning your lighting scheme. Recessed lighting or wall lamps mounted close to work areas can be practical and unobtrusive at the same time.

Light fixtures can be as dressed up or down as you like. Many reproduction fixtures are available with either a tarnish-free or a polished brass finish (the latter requires periodic polishing to maintain its shine). Lampshades are available in a variety of styles with brass trim, scalloped edges, swirl designs, or cone shapes. Popular colors in the Victorian-inspired kitchen include crystal or clear, white, and green.

A High Style Victorian kitchen will be enhanced by using brass fixtures with rich, colorful glass shades. A more subtle approach is best achieved by using white or crystal glass fixtures, or lamps with old-time style and charm. With so many choices available it's wise to first consider the style of lighting you prefer and then plan accordingly to meet your individual needs.

Opposite: In typical Victorian fashion, this quaint kitchen has been outfitted with a beautiful brass hanging fixture sporting scallop-edged glass shades. Stylized floral wallpaper recalls the late-nineteenth-century taste for nature motifs, while rich wood cabinetry and colorful collectibles add Victorian color, pattern, and texture.

Below: The modern convenience of this kitchen is softened by subtle Victorian design. Lace panels at the window filter light and contribute turn-of-the-century charm.

WINDOW TREATMENTS

Early Victorian kitchen windows in urban areas were given little thought or consideration in regard to dressings or curtains, and were frequently left bare. Rural kitchens, where the housewife was more likely to spend a lot of time, may have been treated to gingham or simple muslin curtains.

As household experts began campaigning for cheerful kitchens during the late Victorian period, window shades appeared in the kitchen or cotton rod-pocket curtains were hung and tied back to take advantage of natural light. Another popular window treatment during the 1890s and early 1900s was simple dotted Swiss panels hung on the lower half of the window. They filtered light, afforded privacy, and added a gentle touch to the starkness of the sanitary kitchen.

Taking full advantage of the best of Victoriana, today's kitchen is enhanced by using any number of nineteenth-century window treatments. Painted or stained louvered shutters can add a crisp, clean look to a High Style Victorian kitchen or soft lace panels hung to windowsill length can temper the formality of rich woods and the sharp lines of modern appliances. A dressy valance may be all that's needed at a window in a more formal setting, and the fabric can be coordinated with a wall covering or linens.

Lace is, of course, adaptable to any kitchen and can successfully provide a bridge between old and new in a modern, eclectic, or country decorating scheme. Translucent cotton (sheers), lace, or muslin are ideal for creating cased curtains with a center tie that draws the curtain inward.

Shades are as functional as they were a hundred years ago, and fabric Roman shades with their pleated, tailored look can be an excellent choice for a kitchen window when something other than a curtain is desired.

FURNISHINGS

When household experts wrote about furnishing the Victorian kitchen in home manuals and cookbooks in the nineteenth century, they were referring to the variety of free-standing cupboards and worktables that served specific functions. They also included the numerous items of cookware, gadgets, and utensils used in the kitchen, as well as the cast-iron range and, later, the icebox.

The early Victorian kitchen with massive cooking hearth was outfitted with a sturdy worktable and an open-shelf, step-back cupboard or corner cupboard that held the precious collection of dishware. A pantry lined with shelves stored staples, preserves, and

An integral part of the kitchen during the nineteenth century, the pantry was a necessity in an age before built-in cupboards and modern refrigerators. The pantry seen here is home to a variety of kitchenware items, all of which were stored in the pantry of days gone by, along with sundry food items.

extra cookware, and also served as a cool spot in which to store perishables. As homes grew larger, kitchen space was expanded to incorporate additional service areas such as the scullery and wash or laundry room. In addition, increasingly formal and elaborate dinners called for an enormous amount of china and linens, and extra cookware was needed for the cast-iron range or stove. As a result, more cupboards were called for in the kitchen and a linen press was often used to

safekeep tablecloths, napkins, and so on. With water being pumped into the kitchen, first from the well or large holding containers which collected rain water, the dry sink (a soapstone, iron, or granite sink encased in a low wooden cupboard with storage space below the basin) became a kitchen necessity. Pie safes (enclosed cupboards with wire mesh or punched-tin doors that allowed air to circulate around baked goods) were found in many early Victorian kitchens as were jelly cupboards, which were used to store preserves and valuable spices.

By the late Victorian era, the oak icebox could be found in almost every kitchen and the new focus on sanitary measures made open shelving in the kitchen obsolete. Free-standing cupboards with solid-wood doors or glass-front doors were now favored, and the pantry was equipped with a combination of shelves and tall, built-in cupboards with glass doors or beaded-board paneled doors to protect contents from dust, germs, and vermin. While architects and builders gave little thought to kitchen plans (with the exception of the placement of the stove) through the 1860s, during the last quarter of the century they routinely considered the most convenient location for the icebox and sink as well as the stove, and home building plan books clearly identified space for the butler's pantry, food pantry, and laundry areas. Kitchens were also being constructed with limited built-in cupboards, and the worktable, along with a marble-top pastry table, was still in use.

During the 1890s, there was a tendency to make the kitchen smaller in an effort to make it more convenient for the housekeeper. By the turn of the century, servants were no longer employed in a large number of middle-class homes (many housewives

resorted to having help come in certain days of the week for laundry or heavy cleaning) and were slowly being replaced by labor-saving appliances and kitchen gadgets advertised as the "new servants." Kitchens in this period were equipped with gleaming white porcelain enamel sinks that stood on tall legs, built-in cupboards that held dishware, and eventually, the modern gas stove. An all-

The dry sink was an important kitchen furnishing during the Victorian era. This beautiful beadboard piece incorporates a scalloped backsplash used to display vintage kitchenware. A Hoosier cupboard can be seen on the left.

purpose, freestanding unit known as a baker's cupboard (we generically refer to them as Hoosier cabinets) was introduced during the 1890s, and these factory-made "helpmates," as they were advertised, included storage cupboards, a pullout work surface of wood or metal, bins for flour, sugar, and cornmeal, and assorted small spice drawers. Often quite elaborate, with frosted or

etched-glass cupboard doors, these cabinets were designed as one-stop food preparation centers and were popular for use in homes and apartments or flats.

Round or square oak tables and pressed-back chairs were found in the late-nineteenth-century kitchen for breakfast, lunch, and informal family dinners.

When we discuss furnishing the Victorian Revival kitchen, our thoughts turn to appliances, built-in kitchen cabinets, and the continuous countertop that provides us with a much-needed work area. Appliances need not be hidden, but nor should they take center stage. White, almond, or black appliances with clean lines can blend beautifully in a kitchen displaying distinct nineteenth-century style.

Cabinetry is available in stock or custom-crafted units with an extensive selection of laminates, woods, finishes, and hardware to choose from. A High Style Victorian kitchen can be outfitted with gleaming white cabinets featuring brass pulls and trim; rich cherry, pine, hickory, or oak cabinets with a dark stain will recall the subtle elegance of the old-fashioned butler's pantry. Many manufacturers offer tambour doors for countertop storage areas, leaded glass or colored glass inserts for cabinet doors, decorative crown moldings, and fancy fretwork designs that can be combined with cabinetry in any number of ways.

Streamlined cabinetry in the modern or eclectic kitchen can evoke Victorian spirit with simple glass doors or with something as subtle as brass, glass, or porcelain knobs or pulls. A country kitchen is ideal for golden oak cabinets or with painted stock cabinets. The Victorians frequently painted pantry cupboards or built-in kitchen cupboards to match their walls.

Above: This country kitchen goes Victorian by introducing a vintage cast-iron range with decorative metal trim. The result is a potpourri of contemporary and nineteenth-century pieces, creating a warm and homey atmosphere.

Opposite: In creating today's Victorian-inspired kitchen, custom cabinetry can recall the free-standing cupboards found in kitchens of the last century. Function and style combine to lend an old-fashioned flavor to this polished yet practical setting.

If new cabinets are out of the question and you're looking for a creative way to give your present cabinets a Victorian feel, changing knobs or pulls can have surprising impact. Go one step further by simply replacing cabinet doors to give your kitchen an entirely new look—consider a beadboard door design, which is very similar in appearance to wainscoting.

There are more choices for a truly beautiful and serviceable countertop than you might imagine. Depending upon your remodeling or building budget, you can invest in granite or marble countertops, which are authentic Victorian materials, or you can opt for a tile counter, which also conveys nineteenth-century spirit. Any of these would be the perfect touch in a High Style kitchen where the richness of design elements creates a more formal atmosphere.

chairs in Victorian style: a drop-leaf or gate-leg table in a beautiful, deep wood tone will complement a High Style kitchen very nicely while an oak set can comfortably blend into any design scheme. Something fun and unusual can also offer great visual impact, such as a vintage ice cream parlor table and chairs or a light and airy wicker set. For a finishing touch a large kitchen can usually accommodate a vintage cupboard for authentic flair.

DECORATIVE ACCESSORIES AND COLLECTIBLES

Victorian style can take center stage in today's kitchen by making use of the colors, designs, furnishings, and vintage materials (or modern look-alikes) that were in vogue throughout the nineteenth century, but to add that personal touch to your kitchen and give it a truly customized look, you'll want to decorate with accessories and collectibles.

In the 1860s, Catharine Beecher and Harriet Beecher Stowe encouraged women to make their kitchens cheerful by placing plants at kitchen windows. Since the Victorians were enthusiastic gardeners both indoors and outdoors, flowers and greenery were always welcome in the kitchen, adding freshness and natural beauty.

Even though the Victorian kitchen was mainly a utilitarian space, the nineteenth-century tendency to embellish even the most mundane household article lent quaint charm to this labor-intensive area. For example, the mass-produced cast-iron gadgetry that flooded the shops by the late 1860s was routinely decorated with floral or foliage designs, incised lines, or even animal heads, which were commonly featured on nutcrackers. In personalizing your kitchen with antique gad-

A less costly alternative to the natural materials mentioned is plastic laminate, available in countless colors and patterns, some of which offer the look of marble or granite. High-tech Dupont Corian is more expensive than laminates but is stain resistant and virtually indestructible. Such solid plastics are also available in every color imaginable and in numerous designs that create Victorian atmosphere with the convenience of modern materials.

Butcher-block counters are usually associated with the rural or country kitchen, where they remind us of the old-fashioned chopping block or well-worn worktable. The country Victorian kitchen is the ideal setting for as much or as little of this effect as you'd like. Butcher block is ideal for a center island

This charming kitchen studded with Victorian accents is given a dose of formality by incorporating a faux marble countertop. A stylized tile floor and warm wood cabinets complete with white porcelain knobs contribute additional nineteenth-century flavor.

or as an insert in your counter for a food-preparation area. Be aware that butcher block requires periodic treatment with a non-toxic oil such as tung oil.

Don't overlook outfitting your kitchen with an antique or reproduction table and

gets and utensils, focus on the factory-made goods of the late nineteenth century, such as coffee mills, cherry stoners, brass scales, ceramic trivets, or pewter ice cream molds, and leave the woodenware, such as butter molds or butter churns and primitive utensils, to country-decorating aficionados.

Vintage cookware can be striking when displayed in a High Style Victorian kitchen. Rich and elegant-looking copper pots and pans, teakettles, and attractive molds remind us of the "uptown" Victorian kitchen, where copper was favored over cast-iron because it was lighter in weight. It was also costly and therefore generally reserved for the kitchens of the well-to-do.

Vintage graniteware (utilitarian kitchen and cookware items of enamel over cast iron

Right: Antiques and collectibles add warmth and personality to the kitchen. Vintage packaging tins such as these were chromolithographed with appealing colors and graphics that lend old-fashioned charm to contemporary settings.

Below: This inviting room mixes freshly painted vintage chairs with cut flowers, a lace tablecloth, and shelves of ceramics. The wallpaper treatment adds soft color and design, while the old-fashioned icebox recalls the simplicity of days gone by.

and later sheet steel) is often associated with the country kitchen, where its vibrant speckled, mottled, or swirled designs add a goodly dose of color, but nineteenth- and early twentieth-century French and European enamelware is also well suited for display in the Victorian Revival kitchen. Differing from their American counterpart in color, graphics, and style or shape, many European-made coffee biggins (which resemble a teapot but have a middle section that filters water through coffee), measuring pitchers, utensils and corresponding racks, teapots, canister sets, and so on were decorated in imitation of ceramics. Hand-painted designs, stenciled designs, transfer prints and later decals featuring nature-inspired birds, butterflies, floral bouquets, or wreaths were quite common during the last years of the nineteenth century. German enamelware often featured rustic roses, and in France garlands of small roses enhanced with gold trim were favored. In contrast, other European countries decorated enamelware with blue designs such as those found on Delft tiles, which were associated with cleanliness. While manufacturers

in the United States were turning out graniteware in gray, brown, blue, or red during the late 1800s, European factories favored colors such as iris, terra-cotta, brown-black, and the ever-popular white with blue trim, which looked like china.

Germany, France, England, Belgium, Austria, and what are now Poland, Slovakia, and the Czech Republic exported large quantities of decorative enamelware to the United States during the last quarter of the nineteenth century into the early twentieth century. European pieces are often mixed in with American-made graniteware at antiques shows and shops, but you can refer to the source directory for information on dealers specializing in antique European enamelware.

No Victorian kitchen was complete without the array of pottery mixing bowls needed to whip up the variety of dishes called for in serving everyday meals as well as the more elaborate dinners for special occasions. Victorians readily embraced machine-made goods, and yellowware, so called because the clay used to create such goods turned yellow once fired, was extremely popular during the second half of the nineteenth century and well into the twentieth. Most yellowware was produced at pottery houses in Ohio and available items included sets of nesting bowls (which could be stacked one inside the other), teapots, molds, rolling pins, custard cups, pitchers, canisters, and so on. The earliest yellowware pieces were quite plain with little or no embellishment. By the mid-century period yellowware was decorated with white, brown, green, or blue bands of color, or a Rockingham glaze was applied, giving the pottery a mottled brown appearance. Molded floral designs or incised lines were being used to enhance yellowware by

the late 1800s, often in combination with bands of color. For the collector smitten by the charm of old pottery, today's Victorian-inspired kitchen is the perfect setting for a display of yellowware, especially bowls, which are readily available for collecting and clearly convey the Victorians' penchant for combining utility with beauty.

Accessorizing the Victorian kitchen with antiques and collectibles is a highly personal form of expression. Victorian treasures are in abundant supply and can be used in creative ways. For example, antique linen tea towels hung in the kitchen are a subtle reminder of days gone by, or a carefully orchestrated display of Victorian packaging tins can pay tribute to growing nineteenth-century industries. Many old chromolithographed containers (such as tea tins) are simply beautiful. Hand-painted plates can create an elegant focal point when hung on a wall or displayed in an antique cupboard....There are endless possibilities; however, keep in mind that unlike the parlor with its carefully crafted clutter, the truly Victorian kitchen is sleek and even a bit formal. Accessorize with restraint and keep the clean look Victorians thought of as "sanitary" to recall authentic nineteenth-century fashion.

———— ✦ ————

Old-world charm and Victorian design happily coexist in this eating area where treasured collectibles take center stage. Richly colored pottery, an antique birdcage, dried flowers, and an iron rooster add character to the room, and an unusual vintage cupboard is both practical and decorative.

CHAPTER FIVE

The Victorian Bathroom

The comfort and convenience we enjoy in the modern bathroom is due to Victorian ingenuity

and ambitious nineteenth-century industrial growth.

Spacious early in the Victorian period, with roomlike furnishings and appointments, the bathroom evolved into

a model of efficiency in the late 1800s, and has basically remained the same in form and function these past

one hundred years. We have even reverted today to making bathrooms roomy and elegant in typical Victorian

fashion—a special place in which to linger in a stress-relieving bath or dally over one's morning toilette.

The Victorians were proud of this new indoor facility and not adverse to showing it off. Read

on to uncover the bathroom's history and development as well as inspiring ideas for re-creating a

luxurious Victorian bath all your own.

This picture-perfect Victorian Revival bath combines old-fashioned fixtures with a crisp, clean tile floor
and dado. Elegant artwork, green plants, and a gilt mirror flanked by wall sconces flavor the setting with
a touch of nineteenth-century formality.

The History of the Victorian Bathroom

It was only a matter of time before inventive Victorians found a way to replace the old outhouse and the bathing accoutrements usually housed in the dressing room with a convenient "water closet," or bathroom. The well-to-do were the first to take advantage of this novel concept, but by the 1860s a bathroom could be found in the majority of middle-class urban homes. This was an era in which a thorough knowledge of etiquette signified good breeding. Personal hygiene was of paramount importance in the late Victorian era and was closely tied to self-respect as well as common consideration for others. As such, bathing was a topic routinely discussed in etiquette manuals. Along with the daily toilette, frequent bathing was recommended as were periodic "air-baths," which exposed the body to air and sunlight for short durations.

When indoor plumbing was introduced in the mid-century, a bedroom was usually converted into a bathroom, and occasionally a smaller bath was carved out of space on the first floor near the kitchen as well. To avoid offending delicate Victorian sensibilities, the bathroom was politely treated as simply another room to be furnished, and opulent darkwood enclosures and case pieces masked the function of tubs, toilets, sitz baths, bidets, and sinks. As was fashionable in the other

"Cleanliness is the outward sign of inward purity. Cleanliness of the person is health, and health is beauty. The bath is consequently a very important means of preserving the health and enhancing the beauty. It is not to be supposed that we bathe simply to become clean, but because we wish to remain clean. Cold water refreshes and invigorates, but does not cleanse, and persons who daily use a sponge bath in the morning, should frequently use a warm one ... for cleansing purposes. When a plunge bath is taken .... Soap should be plentifully used, and the flesh-brush applied vigorously, drying with a coarse Turkish towel."

John H. Young, A.M.
Our Deportment, *1882*

Incorporating a vintage or reproduction porcelain sink complete with old-fashioned taps is a perfect way to invite the past into the modern bathroom. A richly colored wallpaper and small touches like the decorative glass bottles on the table complete the look.

rooms during the 1870s and 1880s, the bathroom was outfitted with beautiful Oriental or needlepoint rugs carefully laid atop the wooden flooring, and walls were routinely embellished with wainscoting, wallpaper, tiles, decorative cornices, and, in some homes, ceiling adornments. As with any room the Victorians took great pride in, artwork was hung in the bathroom to give it a polished look, and fancy marble surfaces and brass hardware made it appear elegant.

By the last decade of the nineteenth century the Victorian obsession with sanitary measures, which influenced the kitchen's laboratorylike appearance, had carried over into the bathroom. Wood casements for tubs, sinks, and toilets vanished in favor of easy-to-clean porcelain fixtures and exposed pipes. All of this was done to ensure cleanliness and therefore victory in the constant battle against germs and disease. That does not imply a lack of ornamentation in the 1890s bathroom, as toilets were cast with appealing molded designs and sinks were adorned with flowing curves in their pedestal bases. Even the bathtub, which had routinely been encased in darkwood paneling, was elegant in its porcelain enamel, claw-foot form. Wooden flooring and rich Oriental rugs were replaced by tile flooring—shining and clean. And as in the kitchen, a wooden wainscot was often replaced by a tile dado. Brass, porcelain, or nickel-plated hardware continued to contribute elegance, and gilt mirrors, artwork, cut-glass perfume bottles, and a touch of greenery from a plant or two kept the late-Victorian-era bathroom beautiful as well as functional.

A rich darkwood sink enclosure pays tribute to the well-dressed bath of days gone by. A gallerylike selection of artwork hung throughout the room conveys instant elegance and imparts a High Style tone.

The bathrooms incorporated into new home designs at the turn of the century were more compact than earlier bathrooms, their function taking precedence over ornamental touches in an era marked by simplified rooms and a back-to-basics mentality.

Creating a Victorian Bathroom

As in the kitchen, we call forth the best of Victorian style to create a bathroom with either subtle or obvious nineteenth-century flavor. A single decorative element or myriad Victorian details will leave no doubt your inspiration was derived from the Gilded Age.

The High Style bathroom sports the elegance of rich darkwoods, pattern in the form of scatter rugs or tile flooring, and crisp porcelain fixtures with gleaming brass hardware. Provided there's enough space, a vintage piece of furniture in a handsome Renaissance Revival style can enhance the Victorian decor, or an elegant gilt mirror can have a sumptuous effect.

Streamlined but no less striking, the turn-of-the-century sanitary bathroom can easily be recreated with the use of tile, a claw-foot tub, and a pedestal sink. This is the Victorian bathroom most of us are familiar with, since many older homes still have claw-foot tubs, which are also easily located through salvage emporiums. In addition, several companies that specialize in reproduction hardware and plumbing fixtures offer new claw-foot tubs and shower accessories.

The country Victorian bath calls to mind delicate pastels, light and airy wicker trimmings, and oak or pine furnishings.

Even the modern, state-of-the-art bathroom or the more eclectic-style bath can recall period charm with natural materials such as wood or marble, a lace window dressing, or perhaps one striking detail, such as a vintage lighting fixture.

It's surprisingly easy to create a Victorian-style bath: the only difficulty lies in choosing from among the vast selection of furnishings or fixtures, wall treatments, flooring, and so on. Outfit your bath to meet your individual needs, keeping in mind wear and tear and how much attention you wish to devote to upkeep.

WALL TREATMENTS

By the 1880s, when bathrooms were commonly found in both urban and more rural homes, they were lavishly decorated in the styles of the day. Walls were treated to an inviting shade of paint in deep, rich tones of red, blue, green, or brown, and often matched or complemented an adjoining bedroom. They may have simply been painted or accompanied by a wooden wainscot. In addition, a sanitary wallpaper (a paper coated with varnish so it could be wiped down) was frequently used in tandem with a wainscot or as a border to achieve a frieze effect. Popular wallpaper patterns included stylized foliage designs or patternwork that imitated tile. Elaborate wall treatments of rich color, art tiles, or handsome woods helped contribute to the furnished look in the Victorian bathroom—a room that could rival the opulence of any parlor in the homes of the well-to-do.

As the bathroom became firmly rooted in middle-class homes, the call to simplify, so strongly advanced by reformists, saw bathroom decor shift to a more utilitarian approach. Wallpaper and wainscoting were

Decorative floral tiles and an attractive wallpaper create instant Victorian splendor in this well-appointed bath. A stunning lady's chair, occasional table, lace curtains, and period lighting fixtures make this room beautiful as well as functional.

discarded in favor of sanitary tiles during the 1890s, and tile dados and friezes were combined with crisply painted walls. In addition, delicate stenciled borders often contributed a subtle romantic look.

In creating today's Victorian-inspired bathroom there are almost unlimited options regarding wall treatments. For example, you can achieve a traditional effect by making use of a darkwood wainscot (being sure to treat it with a protective varnish or coat of polyurethane) and a muted-color wallpaper with stylized naturalistic motifs.

If your bathroom is subject to heavy use, you may wish to consider a fabric-backed vinyl wallcovering with stain-resistant and easy-care qualities. Delicate wallpapers such as flocks (which look like velvet) and grass-cloth coverings should be avoided in a room that is routinely exposed to so much moisture. An exhaust fan is really a good idea regardless of your choice in wall coverings.

In an especially small bath or in a room with limited lighting, the reflective finish of a foil wallpaper can lend traditional ambience as well as aid in reflecting light.

If the crisp, clean look of the late nineteenth century appeals to you, a tile floor in combination with a tile dado, and even a tile frieze, can be absolutely stunning. There are so many color and pattern choices available that you can create unlimited decorative effects with tile. Start with the basic color — white — and work from there to create geometric designs with accent tiles in striking shades of black, gray, dark green, blue, or even red.

Tongue and groove wainscoting is equally at home in a bathroom reminiscent of the turn of the century, but for a different twist, paint it white or in a shade matching the rest of the walls.

A country Victorian bath is the ideal location for a floral or geometric mini-print wallpaper, especially in a smaller room or half-bath. Walls painted in a light color, with an attractive wallpaper border or stenciled design, are another option.

The modern or eclectic bathroom can recall subtle Victorian style with either deep tones or pastel-painted walls, decorative tiles, or even a modern laminate used as a dado in imitation of tile or marble.

Victorian design is interpreted in creative ways in this handsome bathroom. Wooden wainscoting on walls and tub surround has been dressed with turquoise paint for dramatic effect. The porcelain sink, brass hardware, and eye-catching mirror contribute to the classic appeal of this nineteenth-century design.

FLOORING

Quite simply, the floor in the Victorian bathroom was either wood, tile, or, by the turn of the century, linoleum. When bedrooms or some other space were converted into bathrooms, their wood flooring was retained and dressed with attractive Oriental rugs. By the 1880s, the water-repellent qualities of tile made it the ideal floor covering and the dec-

orative possibilities made it all the more desirable. The sanitary bathroom of the 1890s frequently featured a tile floor, or, particularly in many middle-class homes, the less-expensive linoleum.

Today's Victorian-inspired bath can showcase dramatic results in flooring by taking advantage of hardwoods, tile, or modern resilient flooring.

A hardwood floor is well suited to a traditional High Style bathroom, provided it's been stained and sealed or coated with a protective polyurethane finish. If your bathroom is subject to hard use, however, a wood floor is not your best option. You have to be alert to water spills and wipe them up immediately, and your wood floor will no doubt require periodic maintenance (such as waxing if the floor has been treated with a penetrating sealer) to keep it in tip-top shape. The wood floor in a High Style Victorian bathroom appears undressed without an Oriental rug or two, which gives it a finished look.

A country Victorian bathroom is often outfitted with a wood floor, but in this relaxed, informal setting your floor can be "washed" with a light coat of paint to highlight the variety of textures in the wood, or stenciled to create a border design or an artistic "rug" or "floorcloth" in the center of the room.

An all-time favorite in the bathroom, in both the past and present, tile is as functional and durable as it is beautiful. Taking your cue from the Victorians, you can opt for a traditional tile floor featuring small hexagonal or square tiles, or mix and match shapes and colors to create a stunning floor, perhaps with an eye-catching tile border.

Tile is equally suitable in a modern or eclectic bath where waterproof properties are important, and you can create virtually any pattern, design, or color scheme to match or contrast with the rest of your decor.

An effective alternative to tile is vinyl flooring. Whether laid in sheet form or in twelve-by-twelve-inch (30.4 by 30.4cm) squares, this resilient flooring allows you to create the look of tile, marble, or wood without the expense, and vinyl is relatively easy to maintain. For the bathroom subjected to heavy wear and tear you may want to consider sheet vinyl rather than the squares, in order to avoid having numerous seams that could be damaged by exposure to water from the tub, shower, and so on.

CEILINGS

Very elaborate Victorian bathrooms sometimes featured a decorative ceiling medallion, but more common treatments included a decorative pressed-tin ceiling, eye-catching moldings, stenciled designs, or wallpaper treatments.

Any of the above can be applied in today's bathroom for a Victorian flair, but a reproduction center medallion is best suited to a spacious, traditional bath featuring all the charm and handsome elegance of rich woods and vintage period accessories, such as an outstanding Renaissance Revival–style mirror, Oriental rugs, frosted glass windows, and noteworthy artwork.

Reproduction pressed-tin ceiling panels, available in a variety of patterns with corresponding ceiling moldings, are most effective coupled with an attractive marble-top or porcelain-enamel pedestal sink, a claw-foot tub, and a generous dose of late-nineteenth-century (or reproduction) brass or porcelain hardware. Pressed-tin ceiling panels can be painted in the color of your choice but are quite attractive in white.

Above: Reminiscent of the sanitary bathroom so popular at the end of the nineteenth century, small hexagonal tiles create a showstopping floor in this spacious room. Victorian flavor is enhanced with a claw-foot tub and a sink enclosure that resembles a case piece of furniture.

Opposite: In late Victorian style, this splendid bathroom has been dressed with a wallpapered ceiling for a unified effect. As the romantic floral design makes its way up the walls and across the room, elegance pervades and creates an inviting retreat for the end of the day.

Decorative stenciled designs can be used to embellish the ceiling in any bath, and your choice of pattern or color can complement the room's decor. While a geometric design

may be ideal in a late-nineteenth-century-style bath with a goodly amount of tile and gleaming porcelain, a soft floral or foliage pattern can accent a country Victorian bath quite nicely.

Wallpaper can be especially beneficial in a small room, where extending pattern up the walls and across the ceiling unites the room and can help soften the angular lines of a slanted roof. Wallpapered ceilings are adaptable to a country Victorian decorating scheme as well as to the Victorian-inspired bathroom reflecting the splendor of the 1880s and early 1890s. Wallpapered ceilings were then very much in vogue, along with the more elaborate tripartite wall treatments.

The most basic treatment, of course, is paint, which has the advantage of being easy to reapply as the moisture of the room takes its toll. A white ceiling will help reflect natural light in the bathroom while a pale or pastel shade gives the illusion of height. In contrast, the room with an extremely high ceiling can be made more intimate by painting the ceiling a darker shade than the walls to lower the ceiling visually.

LIGHTING

The Victorian bathroom was usually illuminated by a hanging ceiling fixture; later, gas wall lamps or sconces were added alongside the mirror over the sink.

The same lighting scheme continues to work well today, and in general, your choice of fixtures will be determined by the level and style of your bathroom's decor. Several companies offer reproduction nineteenth-century fixtures, which are quite at home in the Victorian-inspired bath. Or you may wish to search for authentic lighting fixtures that can be converted for electrical use.

The more formal Victorian bathroom is simply lovely when embellished with brass fixtures sporting frosted or etched-glass globes. A ceiling light is fine, but if your room has a high ceiling you may want to consider a bolder lighting effect such as a vintage or reproduction hanging fixture. Complete the setting with sconces placed on either side of the mirror, and if your bathroom is unusually large, a small lamp with a decorative glass or fabric shade can be placed atop an antique washstand or table.

Follow through with basically the same scheme in bathrooms sporting a crisp, turn-of-the-century look, a country Victorian decor, or modern or eclectic style. Choose fixtures with brass trim to evoke true Victorian spirit, and glass globes, whether white, frosted, colored, or elaborately etched, can be as simple or as decorative as you like.

WINDOW TREATMENTS

Many Victorian bathroom windows were adorned with art glass or, later, frosted glass, which afforded privacy and required little else in the way of window dressing. Plain glass windows, however, were early on covered with venetian blinds, then shutters, shades, or a simple and functional curtain.

The owner of an old house may be fortunate enough to have a decorative window in the bath, but for those who don't, a vintage art-glass window can easily be located through an architectural salvage emporium, or one can be made by a glass studio. This is an especially nice touch in a High Style bathroom but can also serve as a singular design element in a modern or eclectic setting, where the opulence of the window conveys the spirit of the late-nineteenth-century Aesthetic Movement.

Above: In this charming Victorian country bath, wall sconces combine with an overhead fixture draped with a bit of lace to provide soft but ample light. Candlelight is a perfect choice for unwinding in the tub. Note that the ruffled window treatment and matching shower curtain add country-style flavor to this otherwise Victorian setting.

Opposite: Lighting in the Victorian Revival bath can be used to achieve any number of desired effects. This hanging fixture, a frosted glass globe with a floral motif, is well suited to the high ceiling and softens the handsome wood tones of the furnishings.

The contemporary counterpart of venetian blinds, mini-blinds are available in a wide range of colors to match your decor and are well suited to any bath.

Louvered wooden shutters are especially appropriate in a traditional decorating scheme and can be stained to match wood trim and furnishings or painted to match the room's color palette. Shutters are actually adaptable to any bathroom and are ideal in the modern bath without architectural moldings or embellishments.

Shades are available today in simple or more decorative fashions. Functional and unobtrusive when not in use, shades are ideal in the bathroom with a pleasing—and private—view, where little or only occasional window coverage is required.

When a curtain is called for, lace panels (perhaps used in combination with a shade) add to the Victorian decor in a more formal High Style bathroom but can also stand alone and clearly convey nineteenth-century spirit in a modern, eclectic, or country setting. Several notable companies specialize in lace curtains (refer to the source directory) and there are so many beautiful designs and styles available that it can be hard to narrow your choice to just one. Most lace panels, swags, and valances are made in white or natural.

Chintz or a simple cotton curtain is often favored in a country Victorian bathroom, where it can be matched with a sink skirt, shower curtain, tank cover, and so on. Sometimes an elaborate window treatment full of ruffles and trimwork is called into use, and while this is fine in a country Victorian bathroom, it would be too fussy in a formal or turn-of-the-century room, where restrained elegance and beauty were the keys to admirable Victorian style.

FURNISHINGS

Before a room was set aside in the home for a proper bathroom, the dressing room (adjoining the bedroom) served as an area for the daily toilette, and portable bathtubs were set up here for a cleansing "wet bath" at least once a week. The dressing room contained a commode or small, chestlike case piece, which held the chamber pot along with a basin and pitcher, or a commode was accompanied by a separate washstand with a pottery or enamelware basin, towel bar, and a shelf underneath to hold the pitcher. The man's dressing room also included a shaving stand. Every morning hot water was laboriously transported upstairs by the chambermaid and her work included the particularly unpleasant task of emptying and cleaning the chamber pots.

As the bathroom evolved, these familiar furnishings were moved to this new area, but it wasn't long before a cohesive style began to emerge in the bathroom, and during the late nineteenth century, bathrooms were furnished in the true sense of the word. Columned, bracketed, and adorned with moldings, crests, and pediments, wood enclosures or casements that house the toilet,

Opposite: Delicate lace panels are used in tandem with an elegant swag to dress the bathroom window; bits of stained glass bring vibrant color and pattern to an otherwise simple treatment. Thought sanitary by the Victorians, the tile background here is warmed by the addition of decorative artwork and myriad accessories.

Left: Creative measures can produce beautiful results. Here a ceramic sink embellished with a striking floral design has been juxtaposed with a rustic birch-bark vanity. The lushness of Victorian design is tempered by the ruggedness of an Adirondack camp theme.

tub, and sink made these utilitarian fixtures appear handsome and elegant—form was elaborate while function was subtly masked. This trend continued through the 1880s, and plumbing catalogs of the era illustrated and offered everything from brass faucets to walnut, cherry, or ash casings for toilets (the toilet casing was actually chairlike), tubs, and sinks. The casing for sinks was almost dresser style, with a rich marble top, a recessed sink, and a large mirror with shelves. Storage space below the sink served not only to hide the plumbing but provided an area for toiletries, towels, and so on.

Changing styles influenced bathroom decor, and by the 1890s the sanitary bath had emerged, with sparkling white furnishings or fixtures sporting very little wood. Claw-foot tubs may have retained a wooden molding

"Bathrooms are no longer a novelty in small towns and farmhouses. But it must be understood that to enjoy these in winter, requires almost of necessity a range or furnace....When possible, cover the floor of the bathroom with tile....Hang the walls with waterproof paper...or hang India matting three feet [0.9m] high around the wall above the wainscot boards, and finish top and bottom with a small piece of molding....The best plumbing and porcelain are none too good for the bathroom."

Sidney Morse
Household Discoveries, 1908

marble or china sinks supported by narrow, spindled legs. Molded designs or hand-painted decorations were commonly featured on these fixtures.

In creating a Victorian-inspired bathroom, you can draw on the expertise of any of several companies that specialize in reproduction fixtures. Also, noted manufacturers have begun producing lines of tubs, sinks, and toilets with vintage appeal.

The homeowner with a genuine late-nineteenth-century bathroom that hasn't been subjected to remodeling can often have old fixtures brought back to life through a reglazing process, regardless of whether they are made of porcelain, vitreous china, ceramic tile, or cultured marble.

Victorian enthusiasts are employing a myriad of creative measures to outfit the more formal, traditional bath. Antique furnishings and vintage materials are assessed for use in the bathroom: a Renaissance Revival–style dresser with an elegant marble top can be fitted with a sink or two; a whatnot shelf may serve as a display of toilet articles or towels; a tub can be encased with a wood surround that's been given a rich, dark stain and then varnished; tiles may be used to create a tub casement and, depending upon your choice of colors, can have an eye-catching, dramatic effect; an occasional table can hold pretty bath accessories; or an upholstered chair can be introduced for comfort.

For those desiring the "sanitary" bath that recalls the turn-of-the-century period, nostalgic fixtures are readily available in a wide variety of styles, including decorative pedestal sinks, wall-mounted sinks, and wall-mounted corner sinks, which are ideal in the tiny half-bath. A ceramic or brass drop-in sink basin placed in a vintage dresser, sideboard, or marble-top table provides an art-

ful, yet handsome, solution. Reproduction toilets with attractive molded designs and even sets with a wooden wall tank and pull-chain create a truly authentic Victorian look.

Cast-iron claw-foot tubs with roll tops or slipper backs (a raised back for comfortable, luxurious soaks) are another classic turn-of-the-century bathroom feature. Solid brass or plated brass claw feet or unfinished cast-iron feet that can be painted to match the tub are distinctive touches, while handheld or circular shower attachments, gleaming brass hardware, and a brass tub basket for soap and sponges complete your claw-foot tub.

Don't overlook the smaller accents that can strengthen the vintage appearance of your bath—brass or porcelain towel rings and bars, tissue holders, soap dishes, and cup holders can all express Victorian spirit. If space allows, include a wicker chair, a vintage hanging cupboard, or a handsome nineteenth-century dresser for added charm and extra storage.

The country Victorian bath can borrow many of the ideas mentioned to recall days gone by, but rather than accessorizing with brass, use porcelain hardware for a softer look. Dress up a wall-hung sink with fabric skirting (which can match curtains), and consider painting a claw-foot tub in an attractive shade or with a hand-painted floral design. If the bathroom is large enough, putting an antique pine cupboard or a quaint

The claw-foot tub is quintessential to the Victorian bath. An austere white background and accessories recall the sanitary nineteenth-century bath with stunning beauty.

around the top, and toilets had a wooden tank (high up on the ceiling with a pull-chain to flush), seat, and lid, but the wooden casements were now passé. Hardware was brass or porcelain, and plumbing for the toilet, sink, and tub were exposed for easy cleaning. Pedestal-style sinks were popular, along with

cottage-style dresser to work as a storage area enhances subtle rural charm.

A modern or eclectic bath can feature a stunning pedestal sink for old-time flair, or simply using High Style brass hardware will capture a bit of the Victorian past.

"The washstand should be furnished with a large bowl and pitcher, small pitcher and tumbler, soap-tray, sponge-basin, holding two sponges (large and small), china tray containing two tooth-brushes and nail brushes, and a bottle of ammonia. On the right of the wash-stand should be the towel-rack, which should contain one fine and two coarse towels and two more very coarse...Turkish towels. The foot-bath should be placed beneath the washstand."

Richard A. Wells, A.M.
Manners, Culture and Dress of the
Best American Society, *1891*

DECORATIVE ACCESSORIES AND COLLECTIBLES

Once your Victorian-inspired bath is outfitted, you'll want to add that personal touch by introducing the subtle beauty of plants and flowers (ferns do especially well in the bathroom), putting favorite collectibles on display, and dressing the walls with framed prints or artwork.

Many of the items originally sold with nineteenth-century chamber "wash sets," including washbowl, pitchers, chamber pots, or toothbrush holders, can become decorative elements in today's nostalgic bath. A beautiful ceramic or European enamelware washbowl and pitcher adorned with a floral or foliage motif can be placed atop a vintage chest or cupboard. Use delicate ceramic toothbrush holders as originally intended or group an eye-catching collection of these pieces on a display shelf.

Items included in Victorian dresser sets can also be collected and displayed in the bathroom. China or pressed-glass cologne bottles, puff boxes, rose bowls, or hairpin boxes, with their dainty size and attractive design work, make a stunning display in the bathroom. Simply having three of something creates a collection and gives dramatic effect in a small setting, so don't let the diminutive size of the bathroom discourage you from showing off your antiques and collectibles.

Use old baskets to hold towels or magazines and give small, hand-painted bowls or dishes new life as soap dishes and fragrant potpourri containers.

As a perfect finishing touch, hang art in the Victorian-style bath for a friendly yet polished look. While a more formal bath is the ideal setting for a selection of botanical prints in rich, gilded frames, in other Victorian-inspired baths it might be fun to add an

Above: Sundry grooming items, both functional and decorative, make an eye-catching display in the Victorian Revival bathroom. Antique dresser sets, shaving accessories, pillboxes, and the like are easy to collect and put the finishing touch on any countertop or vanity.

Opposite: Color, material, or function can unify a collection. Here, ring boxes, potpourri boxes, and compacts, all in silver, line up beneath a splashy floral wallpaper for a pretty, tasteful display.

unexpected twist such as a fine art print, a nostalgic poster, framed sheet music or magazine covers, or old trade cards advertising soap or toiletries.

CHAPTER SIX

The Victorian Bedroom

Private spaces devoted to rest and relaxation, Victorian bedrooms are today viewed as unabashedly romantic retreats. In appraising the subtle charms of the old-fashioned boudoir, we treasure the cozy fireplaces, large, inviting beds, massive dressers with elegant mirrors and marble tops, sundry grooming items, sentimental photographs, and other cherished possessions. We can picture ourselves reclining on a plush fainting couch engrossed in a good novel while surrounded by nineteenth-century luxuries that make us feel pampered and secure.

Escape to the Victorian bedroom, where practicality mingles with the decorations of a bygone era. Exploring the past provides us with clues to capturing the essence of the bedchamber—a room for rest, relaxation, and whatever else you might want it to be.

Combining all the elements of a High Style Victorian bedroom, this opulent room features papered walls and a decorative cornice, a period lighting fixture, handsome furnishings, and a room-sized carpet layered with plush area rugs. Note, too, that the sumptuous bed dressing includes a whimsical crazy quilt for added nineteenth-century charm.

The History of the Victorian Bedroom

As homes grew larger during the early nineteenth century, bedrooms, commonly referred to as "chambers," were located on the second and third floors of Victorian homes. The family members occupied the larger rooms on the second floor at the front of the house, while servants had small rooms located toward the back or on the atticlike third floor accessible via a rear stairway located off the kitchen.

Early in the Victorian period the tall four-poster bed was shrouded in canopies that helped keep the cold night air at bay. But the canopied bed and a variety of other furnishings were replaced by matching

Opposite: Bands of brocade and swaths of gold give this lavish canopy and these bed hangings an ultrarich look. The sumptuous effect is enhanced by gilt trim and florettes on the wooden valance and gilt frames on the trio of nineteenth-century landscapes.

Below: Often outfitted with a potpourri of furnishings, the Victorian bedroom acquired a cozy, lived-in charm. A comfy chaise longue is perfectly suited to the relaxing atmosphere of this bedchamber, where the piece blends beautifully into the old-fashioned setting.

bedroom suites during the mid-century period, and ornate Rococo Revival or Renaissance Revival furniture was featured in the chambers of the well-to-do. Many middle-class Victorians took advantage of the less-costly factory-made spool beds and cottage furnishings to outfit their private rooms. In another cost-saving measure, castoffs from the parlor, such as chairs or settees, frequently found a new home in the bedroom.

The dressing room portion of the bedroom served as a bathroom of sorts until the proper bath was introduced (in rural areas this was often as late as the early 1900s), and this dressing area included a washstand, a

"The bedroom should be essentially clear of everything that can collect and hold dust in any form; should be bright and cheerful, pleasantly furnished with light and cheerful furniture of good and simple design, in which everything should be carefully arranged for use, not show."

Richard A. Wells, A.M.
Manners, Culture and Dress of the
Best American Society, *1891*

commode, a decorative screen for privacy, and other items needed for the daily toilette.

While the upper middle class or the wealthy often had bedrooms that could rival the splendor of the parlor or the dining room, the bedrooms of the majority of middle-class Victorians were on a more modest scale, though no less attractive.

During the second half of the nineteenth century, proper ventilation of chambers became a topic of significant concern. In their book *The American Woman's Home*, household experts Catharine Beecher and Harriet Beecher Stowe went to great lengths to inform women of the dangers surrounding poorly ventilated rooms. They wrote, "There is a prevailing prejudice against night air as unhealthful to be admitted into sleeping-rooms, which is owing wholly to sheer ignorance."

The need for pure night air to avoid disease and the concern over a healthy environment in the bedroom coincided with the introduction of simplified, reform movement styles in furnishings and design. Always feminine with regard to decoration and personal

The very essence of Victorian design, this striking iron bed combines the light, airy effect so desired during reform movements with the nineteenth-century penchant for fine detail. The ornate scrollwork is enhanced with beautiful floral medallions set into the headboard and footboard. The flower motif is picked up in the wallpaper and carried to the fabric for the bed skirt and the headboard dressing.

"Chambers and bedrooms are of course a portion of the house to be sedulously and scrupulously attended to, if either health or comfort are aimed at in the family. And first, every mistress of a family should see, not only that all sleeping-rooms in her house can be well ventilated at night, but that they actually are so. Where there is no provision made for the introduction of pure air in the construction of the house, and in the bedroom itself no open fire-place to allow the easy exit of foul air, a door should be left open into an entry or room where fresh air is admitted; or else a small opening should be made in a window, taking care not to allow a draught of air to cross the bed. The debility of childhood, the lassitude of domestics, and the ill-health of families, are often caused by neglecting to provide a supply of pure air."

Catharine E. Beecher & Harriet Beecher Stowe
The American Woman's Home, *1869*

touches, bedrooms were now to be light and airy rather than dark and outfitted with carpets, wallpapers, or ornately carved furnishings, which would harbor stale air, germs, or disease. The typical bedroom of the late 1800s featured pale or pastel painted or papered walls (the Victorian love of wallpaper made it difficult to follow the advice against its use in the bedroom) and wood floors with area rugs. Furnishings, although kept to a minimum, were still plentiful by today's standards, and might include several upholstered pieces and a writing desk as well as the bed. Growing awareness regarding sanitary measures dur-

ing the 1890s made brass and iron beds quite popular. Iron beds painted in white enamel were thought to harmonize well with birch, golden oak, or painted furnishings, and brass beds complemented darker walnut or mahogany furniture.

Linen or cotton sheets and blankets were used atop the feather mattress, accompanied by a white spread made of lined lace, dimity, or dotted muslin. Crazy quilts (quilts made of fabric remnants pieced together without a regularized design) or comforters were used for added warmth during the winter months. Bed skirts, commonly referred to as "valances," were not required and in fact were considered unsanitary by some, since they did not allow air to circulate freely under the bed.

Simple but attractive window dressings, rich Oriental rugs, and a medley of furnishings gave the Victorian bedroom a rather romantic look—one we aspire to today.

Creating a Victorian Bedroom

Whether used strictly as a room in which to sleep or also as a sitting area for private rest and relaxation, the Victorian-inspired bed-

"If a house is well built, suitably located, and free from dampness, a bedroom may be on the ground floor, although as a rule one of the upper floors is better. It has been well said that 'a bedroom should be deaf to noise, and blind to light.' It is not always possible to attain this, but it is the object to aim at. The glare of a sunny room may be modified by linen curtains, and a baize covering to the door will deaden sound. The room should be well ventilated, and yet free from draughts. The windows should open from the top, and there should be a fireplace in the room, if possible. A painted and varnished wall is doubtless the best. It is non-absorbent, and is easily cleaned. If papered, let the design be free from any pronounced figures or striking patterns, which, in the half-lights of the night or early morning, will suggest to the tired brain weird figures or mathematical problems. A bedroom should be light rather than dark, and the furniture and general woodwork, such as the doors, wainscoting, etc. should be of light colors. The latter should be varnished so that it can be easily washed and cleaned."

Smiley's Cook Book and New and Complete Guide for Housekeepers, *1898*

room can exhibit all the charm and comfort associated with days gone by. Restrained beauty created with simple wall treatments, rugs, and furnishings can take center stage, or the decor can be more elaborate, with ruffles, masses of lace, and other ornamental embellishments. The bed is generally the focal point of the bedroom, and around this the other historical aspects will convey High Style or subdued Victorian grace.

WALL TREATMENTS

During the Victorian era, chamber walls were painted or papered in shades of color befitting the room's location or exposure to natural light. Sunny rooms were best treated to a light tone such as a pastel pink, blue, or green or a creamy ivory color. Rooms with a northern exposure were considered well suited to deeper shades such as rose, jade, or a rich blue, which would enhance the feeling of repose rather than make walls appear drab and uninviting.

Striped wallpapers were an early-Victorian-period favorite in dressing the walls in the bedchamber, but as the century progressed soft floral or foliage patterns became popular provided they were not too busy. In addition, many of the more prosperous homes featured a darkwood wainscoting in the chambers.

Bedrooms painted in light or pastel tones were often treated to a wallpaper frieze or a decorative, stenciled border.

Today's Victorian-inspired bedroom takes its cue from the nineteenth-century color palette to create a wall treatment that's as lovely as it is inviting and warm. A traditional High Style bedroom—an almost baronial setting—recalls deep-toned colors and sumptuous darkwood furniture suites. Such

a room can be crafted with muted shades of rose, green, blue, or tan and by accenting the walls with a color-coordinated wallpaper frieze. Another alternative is papering the walls with a flocked paper (a two-tone colored paper with a raised, velvetlike texture) for a rich, formal look.

The Victorian bedroom with golden wood tones and perhaps a brass or iron bed or an Eastlake-style bedroom suite is the ideal setting for walls drenched in a pastel pink, soft blue, beige, or sea green color. Embellish the walls with a narrow wallpaper border or a wider frieze—or leave them plain. Wallpaper in a striped, floral, or foliage pattern can be combined with a ceiling paper for a dressy effect.

In typical Victorian fashion, this bedroom has been decorated with a foliage-patterned wallpaper in restful shades of color. Contrast is achieved via the deep, warm tones in the carpet and decorative accessories such as the privacy screen in the corner.

The country bedroom evokes Victorian flair with a delicate mini-print wallpaper pattern featuring favorite country colors such as earth tones or pastel shades for a decidedly romantic look.

For modern- or eclectic-style bedrooms, borrow from the past and treat walls to light or deep shades of rose, blue, tan, or even soft gray. Keep in mind that these are the colors long associated with repose and are quite appropriate in the contemporary bedroom.

FLOORING

Throughout the Victorian era, wood floors were considered more desirable in the bedroom than carpeting. While softwood floors were often painted, hardwood floors were stained or oiled and then varnished. Strips of carpet, area rugs, or matting were used next to the bed as well as in other areas of the room, and rugs were considered, according to one household expert, "fashionable, wholesome, and tidy." Plus, area rugs could easily be removed to be cleaned.

as was a scarlet-and-gray combination or a dark blue carpet with attractive sprays of lily-of-the-valley running through it.

Outfitting today's Victorian bedroom with the timeless beauty of a wood floor adds warmth and texture to this very personal space. Accented with attractive floral-patterned or Oriental rugs, the bedroom takes on a more polished look, courtesy of the rug's color and design. A beautiful area rug can in fact become a focal point in the bedroom. Oriental designs are especially at home in a formal or eclectic setting, while a needlepoint or hooked rug adds charm to a romantic or country Victorian room.

Straw matting, coco matting, or sisal rugs, often consisting of patterned squares sewn together, are still as functional in the bedroom as they were during the late Victorian era. They can be used year-round for a casual, relaxed look and are especially nice in a summer cottage or a getaway cabin, where their no-fuss qualities make them versatile and easy to care for.

With our clean-burning oil, gas, or electric heat and electric lighting, we don't have to battle the constant dirt and soot Victorian homes were subject to from fireplaces,

Floor coverings such as small rugs or bits of carpet were to be darker than the furnishings but in shades that would blend with the overall color scheme of the room. Oriental rugs were quite popular in the Victorian bedroom, as was straw matting, which was sewn together in strips of various widths. Matting was used especially during the summer months, as it contributed an impression of coolness to the bedroom.

If carpeting was used in the nineteenth-century bedroom, the household experts of the late 1800s proposed that it be in a light shade with a bright floral pattern; Victorian carpets, unlike modern carpeting, was never solid colored. Regarding color combinations, one deportment manual circa 1890 counseled that a pink and blue carpet was quite pretty,

Above: The soft pastel colors and elegant floral pattern of this lovely rug contribute a serene quality and polished look to the room.

Opposite: The strong design of this boldly checkered floor and the masculine lines of a large dresser are softened by a ceiling splashed with yellow roses.

Right: Recalling the simplicity of a farmhouse room, the striped rug seen here tempers the formality of the handsome four-poster bed.

coal-burning stoves, and kerosene lamps. In addition, our state-of-the-art vacuum cleaners and shampoo appliances make caring for wall-to-wall carpeting a snap. As a result, carpeting is a popular floor treatment in the bedroom today, and can evoke Victorian charm in bold or subtle ways. A solid-color carpet can be embellished with decorative area rugs for a plush look, or a carpet with a floral or foliage design can be used for a highly romantic look.

A country Victorian bedroom offers a cheerful, nostalgic appeal when a wood or carpeted floor is treated to brightly colored rag rugs or homey hooked rugs with a Victorian theme.

CEILINGS

Since bedrooms did not generally have the tall ceilings found in the rooms on the first floor of the Victorian home, they were subject to minimal decoration or embellishment.

In dressing the bedroom today, we can follow the Victorians' lead and apply a soft, stenciled border around the perimeter of the ceiling or simply highlight the corners with a subtle design.

An attractive molding defining the division of space between the wall and ceiling lends architectural embellishment in a more formal or even modern bedroom. Paint the ceiling in a soft shade—lighter than walls—to increase space visually. A creamy eggshell or ivory white will also do nicely.

Wallpaper can be an effective ceiling treatment in a romantic setting, where it complements the paint color or paper used on the walls. An allover (walls and ceiling) design can be quite attractive in a small bedroom with quirky slants or angles resulting from the roofline dormers.

Opposite: A lanternlike overhead fixture combines with a bedside light and a striking tabletop lamp in front of the window in this Arts and Crafts–style bedroom.

Below: Not only does the stenciled design create a lovely bowerlike effect, but it draws the eye upward, enhancing the overall area of the room.

LIGHTING

The Victorian bedroom was illuminated by firelight, candles, and kerosene lamps or wall sconces. Ceiling fixtures were not typically used in the bedroom, except in urban well-to-do homes.

In lighting today's Victorian-style bedroom, choose lighting fixtures to meet your needs with an eye toward style and design. A ceiling fixture, often accompanied by a fan, is ideal in any room, and plain or decorative glass globes can be selected to match the level of your decor.

prominent examples. Kerosene-style lamps wired for electricity are the perfect touch in a formal, romantic, or even country Victorian bedroom. You can also consider wicker lamps for subtle nineteenth-century charm.

Brass lamps with colored glass globes will add a bolder but uniquely Victorian look in a modern, eclectic, or country setting, and an art-glass lamp is an object to be admired in even the most austere room.

WINDOW TREATMENTS

Windows in the typical Victorian chamber were dressed with a simple, light curtain of cretonne, cheesecloth, dotted Swiss muslin, dimity, or linen taffeta. Such curtains were often trimmed with lace for a more decorative look, and they were commonly hung on poles above the window and tied back with grosgrain ribbons to allow natural light to flood the room.

There were, of course, exceptions to this common practice, especially in the homes of the upper middle class, where a very sophisticated and formal bedroom was treated to a more elaborate window dressing of rich satin, velvet, or silk draperies tied back with cords and tassels.

Venetian blinds, shutters, and shades were also used in the bedroom and provided a means of filtering the sun's rays.

In choosing a window dressing for today's Victorian Revival bedroom you can call upon any number of treatments to create a rich, elaborate effect, a romantic look, or a simple but elegant scheme. A very formal High Style bedroom with handsome dark-wood revival furnishings, Oriental rugs, and deep-toned walls is the most appropriate setting for an opulent window dressing. Luxurious velvet or satin drapes tied back

Sconces with old-fashioned charm can be placed alongside a dressing table or flanking the bed, where they're as functional as they are decorative.

Tabletop lamps can serve as task lighting for reading in bed or illuminate a cozy corner devoted to leisurely pursuits. Whether you choose reproduction lamps or vintage examples, a High Style Victorian bedroom can be dressed up with elaborate lamps sporting frosted or etched-glass shades or fabric shades with a decorative fringe or trimwork. Given the feminine overtones of this Victorian setting, delicate glass or ceramic lamps of modest size are preferred to large,

Above: The generous size of this romantic room makes it the perfect candidate for a variety of lighting sources, including an elaborate ceiling fixture, tabletop lamps, and a wall sconce.

Opposite: In this baronial setting, elegant lace-trimmed curtains are held in place with gleaming brass pins, and a handsome wooden valance echoes the deep wood tones of the window shutters.

Decked with tassels and fringe, these elegant curtains with matching valance add classic beauty in this Victorian Revival bedroom. This light approach to window dressing affords a pleasing view and complements the soft and subtle shades used throughout the room.

with eye-catching tassels can pool on the floor, while an undercurtain of lace or muslin provides privacy and filters light. Another option befitting a High Style Victorian bedroom is floor-length lace panels topped with a sumptuous fabric draped over a rod or pole to create a swag and tails. A valance can be employed for the same effect. Shutters stained in a darkwood tone can be used in combination with drapes or curtains—or simply stand alone.

The romance-inspired bedroom with an ornate brass or iron bed, floral needlepoint

rugs, and soothing pastel painted or papered walls calls for a light touch in window dressing. Cotton, muslin, lace, dotted Swiss, or chintz curtains falling to just window-sill length and scooped back with a fabric tie can be the perfect touch in this simplified setting, and a shade can be added for privacy.

To make your window a focal point, consider using Austrian blinds or balloon shades in a light color or a patterned fabric, which can be coordinated with a matching comforter or spread. The puffy, flounced look these balloon shades take on when raised evokes a truly romantic spirit.

For a country Victorian bedroom, attractive tab curtains in a floral print will recall nineteenth-century style, while lace panels or painted shutters will enhance a modern or eclectic setting where just a taste of Victoriana is the desired effect.

FURNISHINGS

Since the Colonial era, the bedroom had served as an area of multiple functions, and this trend continued throughout the nineteenth century. Not only was the Victorian chamber a room set aside for nightly rest, but it also included a private area known as the dressing room for tending to matters of personal hygiene and for dressing or changing clothes. In addition, many chambers included furnishings for quiet relaxation, such as a comfortable rocker or an upholstered fainting couch and perhaps a sewing stand or a desk for writing notes.

During the early Victorian era, bedrooms featured tall, four-poster canopy beds or American Empire sleigh beds (so called because the flowing curves of the bed resembled the shape of a sleigh). By mid-century, factory-produced bedroom suites were avail-

able, and while the hand-painted or stenciled cottage-style furnishings (and later, factory oak) were employed in many middle-class chambers, the grandeur of the upper middle-class or wealthy Victorian's home made elaborate Rococo Revival or Renaissance Revival suites quite popular.

The typical bedroom suite included the bed, a large dresser with a mirror, and a washstand-commode, which was placed in the dressing room or hidden behind a decorative screen. Other furnishings could be purchased along with the three-piece suite, such as a matching armoire, a nightstand, or a tall chest of drawers.

Factory-made beds had extremely lofty headboards (often reaching to heights of eight feet [2.4m] or more), and cottage-style examples were embellished with beautifully painted floral or foliage motifs, while the more costly period styles crafted from rosewood, walnut, or walnut with burled veneer were adorned with applied floral or pierced carvings, massive crests or pediments, applied moldings, and other fancywork.

When wooden bedsteads fell out of favor in the late 1800s, brass or enamel-painted iron beds, thought to be more sanitary, took center stage in the bedroom. Brass and iron beds were actually available by the late 1870s and were even discussed in Charles Eastlake's landmark book, *Hints on Household Taste*. Eastlake noted the shift away from wooden beds as "a change for the better," and he suggested that iron beds be painted in muted tones such as Venetian red, chocolate, or sage green. It was not until the 1890s, however, that iron beds and beds made of both brass and iron became commonplace in the Victorian chamber, and iron beds were then being painted a crisp white or a soft pastel shade.

Dressers and commodes in the fashionable revival styles were usually outfitted with a rich marble top, and dressers could be quite elaborate with decorative fretwork, applied moldings, corner pilasters, incised carvings, bow-front or serpentine-front drawers, and hand-carved fruit-shaped pulls or grips on drawers. Dressers with swing mirrors topped with pediments or moldings and decks, or smaller drawers, situated on either side of the dresser top were also popular.

Other furnishings commonly found in the Victorian bedroom included a bachelor's chest (a tall chest of drawers with a mirror), a lady's cabinet (a small and narrow cupboardlike piece for hats and gloves), a privacy screen (many with Oriental motifs), hanging cabinets, a chair or two, various tables, a wall-mounted grooming mirror, a freestanding or wall-hung towel rack, and a shaving stand. Because Victorian bedrooms were not generally equipped with closets, a large armoire—and often more than one—was an essential.

In furnishing today's Victorian-inspired bedroom, you'll find that antique pieces are still readily available, but some items, such as cottage-style furniture, have become scarce and costly. A vintage bedroom suite would be a rare discovery—estate sales or auctions are often your best bet for locating a complete set. In many instances, a bedroom can be furnished with pieces in a similar style located one at a time. Dressers and commodes are more plentiful than are antique wooden beds, which often ended up as firewood when stylish metal beds took their place. Remember that the height of an antique headboard must be considered in a newer home with low ceilings, and be aware that Victorian beds were made in single, twin, three-quarter, and double sizes only (each was a standard 75 inches

Recalling the early Victorian period, when American Empire furnishings were in vogue, this handsome sleigh bed is resplendent with its graceful curves. Simple yet elegant window dressings, wall treatment, and furnishings allow the rich wood and clean lines of the bed to take center stage. The chintz-covered chaise offer a comfortable place to curl up with a book, and its patterned plushness provides a counterpoint to the polished wood of the bed frame.

[1.9m] long) and do not always meet modern needs. However, if you have your heart set on an antique bed, seek the services of a professional furniture refinisher, who may be able to alter the bed's frame to accommodate a larger mattress.

When buying antique furniture, check each piece carefully to determine condition and authenticity. Inspect construction methods, the finish or patina, hardware, and the condition of the marble top, if one is present.

If you prefer new furniture in an old style, there are companies that specialize in reproduction Victorian furniture, and noted manufacturers have issued new lines with Victorian flair; refer to the source directory.

The ornate High Style Victorian bedroom is stunning when outfitted with Rococo

A brass or iron bed is also perfectly at home in a cottagelike bedroom, and a subtle blend of wicker, oak, or painted furniture will enhance the cozy, romantic mood.

The country-style bedroom can accommodate a brass or iron bed sans curlicues (which would be reserved for a completely Victorianized room), a spool bed, or a golden oak bed, all of which were long associated with rural Victorian homes. A simple oak dresser with brass pulls, a comfy rocker, and vintage washstand or storage trunk will add a nineteenth-century country flair.

The modern or eclectic bedroom can immediately impart Victorian spirit by making an antique or reproduction brass or iron bed the focal point of the room. A less dramatic approach can make use of a singular element, such as an antique chair or a Victorian screen, to recall days gone by.

DECORATIVE ACCESSORIES AND COLLECTIBLES

In today's Victorian-inspired bedroom it's entirely possible to think small in terms of decorative accessories and collectibles and still have big impact. Family photos, fresh flowers, sumptuous bed covers and pillows, decorative throws, and books are some of the more obvious ways to personalize your private space, but by adding a touch of whimsy through collectibles the bedroom will take on a highly individual, nostalgic air.

Since the Victorian chamber was a private space devoted not only to rest and relaxation, but also to grooming and dressing, it was full of personal items used daily. The mistress of the house and her grown daughters had dressing tables in their boudoirs, grooming altars of sorts, accessorized with myriad items that are today cherished

or Renaissance Revival furnishings. Deep-colored walls and Oriental rugs are complemented by the rich ornamentation and dark wood tones displayed in the revival styles. If room allows, add a plush fainting couch or chaise longue for quiet moments of relaxation, or perhaps a small desk for keepsakes and other personal items.

The bedroom recalling the turn of the century is best outfitted with an eye-catching brass or iron bed, or, in an especially small room, a brass or iron daybed. Ornamented antique examples can be hard to find and modern reproductions expensive, but you can employ a headboard only, which clearly conveys a Victorian air while reducing the cost. Complete this setting with an oak dresser, armoire, or even an old-fashioned commode, which can function as a nightstand.

Above: Lavished with every frill and furbelow, this bedroom is a fitting example of High Style romance at its best. The ornate iron and brass bed is set off by other romantic pieces— a plush upholstered armchair, a beribboned dressing table, and a stunning painted trunk.

Opposite: As the focal point of this minimalist setting, a beautiful iron bed pays tribute to the excellence of Victorian design. This wonderful piece can stand virtually alone and still impart strong nineteenth-century style.

The large dresser contained dressing items or accessories such as jewelry, gloves (often protected in an ornate wooden box), handkerchiefs, fans, parasols, and a selection of hatpins kept handy in a decorative glass or hand-painted china hatpin holder. Wide-brimmed hats were very much in vogue during the late Victorian era. Women often had a variety of hats to match different dresses, and numerous hatpins were needed to keep a hat secure atop one's head. Hatpins were created with attractive tops made of precious stones, silver plate, colored glass, or cloisonné. They were used well into the early 1900s, and because Victorian women had at least several different hatpins on hand they've proved to be very popular collectibles—they're reasonably priced and fairly easy to locate.

No Victorian woman was without small beaded or hand-crocheted purses in which to carry her calling-card case and a vinaigrette containing smelling salts. Vintage bags are other popular collectibles that are quite at home in the bedroom, where they can be clustered on hooks with shawls or hats.

In many Victorian homes the master had his own bedroom, but whether or not he kept

The bedroom is the perfect place for highly personal keepsakes and mementos. Surround yourself with cherished photographs of family and friends for a sense of quiet pleasure; the collection of photos here is accompanied by a striking silver dresser set, fresh flowers, and a beautiful lady's fan—all precious reminders of the Victorian past.

antiques and collectibles. Atop the dressing table were toilet waters in decorative glass bottles, cream jars, brushes, combs, hand-held mirrors, a hair receiver (a glass or ceramic jar for saving hair, which would later be fashioned into jewelry or craftwork),

buttonhooks, hairpins, and a manicure set. Many of these necessary items were sold together in a "toilet set," which was often embellished with beautiful mother-of-pearl, silver or silver plate, or celluloid, which had the look of tortoiseshell.

Right: Accessorized with a brilliant art-glass lamp, tabletop keepsakes, a decorative privacy screen, and a vaseful of flowers, this bedroom exudes romantic Victorian spirit. The window's bamboo shade contributes a hint of the Far East, and the plush easy chair is outfitted with protective and decorative antimacassars.

Below: Often a well-chosen accessory or two is all that's needed to create a homey setting. Sunflowers nodding in a cobalt vase and favorite books stacked on a serving tray add personal charm in this tiny room, while the colorful bedcover and matching tassel on the chest of drawers hint at Victorian restraint.

a separate room, he too required a plethora of items to tend to his own needs and accessorize his outfits. His tall chest of drawers was laden with combs and brushes, a buttonhook and shoehorn, assorted collar buttons and sleeve buttons or cuff links, and a pocket watch and pocketknife. Just as madame had a decorative box on her dresser for gloves, her husband had a box for shirt collars. For social events, she had a parasol, he a wooden cane.

Since we derive so much pleasure and comfort from surrounding ourselves with the things we truly love, most collectors are quite passionate about the items of their interest. Accessorize your bedroom to please yourself. Whether you choose to amass small decorative boxes, hunt down vintage hatpins, or assemble an array of colored-glass perfume bottles, you can display these objects in small groupings that will enchant you each time you enter your chamber.

The Victorian Porch

The porch grew to be much, much more than simply an exterior embellishment or architectural detail during the Victorian era. The porch eventually became a significant part of the home—an extended living area during the warm months and the site of many a casual gathering or festive social function.

Furnishings were designed, created, and chosen with the porch in mind, and decorative accessories in the form of plant stands, flowers, hanging baskets, and lush greenery enhanced the beauty of this relaxed outdoor setting.

Pamper yourself by relaxing in a comfy wicker chair or an old porch rocker. Pour a glass of lemonade, breathe in the fresh summer air, and relish your quiet time. Read on to uncover the history and growing popularity of the porch during the Victorian period as well as decorating ideas that can be borrowed for use today. The porch has come full circle…and is once again on everyone's wish list.

With the benefit of a breathtaking view, little else is needed to enjoy the great outdoors. Casual wicker furnishings are ideally suited to the porch that acts as a well-used extension of the home—an outdoor room of sorts.

The History of the Victorian Porch

During the early Victorian period, gardens were very much in vogue, and the middle and upper classes lavished their landscapes with great care and attention. The wealthy often subscribed to a more formal arrangement in the garden, laying out hedges and flower beds to create geometric designs, while the middle class often opted for a romantic, cottage-style garden. The preference for a profuse, natural mixture of floral and foliage beds was explored by Andrew Jackson Downing in his 1841 book, *A Treatise on the History and Practice of Landscape Gardening,* and was viewed as the ideal landscape for then-popular Gothic Revival–style homes.

The Victorians enjoyed their gardens, and a great many social activities and amusements were conducted on the lawn. Cast-iron furniture in the form of benches, tables, and chairs were ideally suited to the outdoors and perfect for afternoon tea in the garden.

Architectural styles changed throughout the nineteenth century and the covered portico found on many Greek Revival–style

Spacious and airy, this circular porch has been lavishly treated to parlorlike embellishments. Wicker combines with flowers and greenery to provide a relaxing atmosphere, while gorgeous window dressings and an unusual ceiling treatment provide a stunning backdrop.

buildings (1830–1850) provided a covered entryway and classical adornment, but little in the way of extended living space.

Gothic Revival–style homes, popular from the 1840s through the 1860s, often featured piazzas on either side of the front entrance or an ornamental veranda that continued from the front of the house around the side or sides. The piazza or veranda contributed to the picturesque effect of this style, with its emphasis on vertical lines, and was also practical, since the piazza helped keep the house cooler during the warm months.

By the 1860s the Italianate style (also known as American Bracket style) had become popular, and these square, two- or three-story homes with bracketed eaves, arched windows, and cupolas usually included a decorative, full front porch. A highly romantic style, Italianate villas were generally painted in earth tones to blend with the surrounding landscape. As the Civil War ended, industry was pushing full steam ahead, and the hustle and bustle of city life prompted a longing for peacefulness, relaxation, and an escape to nature. Many Victorians began spending part of their summers at seaside resorts, in the mountains, or under the cool shade provided by their own front porches.

While a flower garden remained a high priority for the middle-class homeowner, the prevailing fashion during the late Victorian era shifted to a well-manicured lawn with large trees and walkways bordered by flower beds. Entertaining moved from the garden to the porch, and especially in later nineteenth-century architectural styles such as Stick style (1860–1890), Queen Anne style (1870–1900), and Shingle style (1880–1900), the porch developed a character and a purpose all its own. With Queen Anne homes—

the quintessential Victorian style—the porch often displayed an eclectic mix of curved spaces, with circular areas located at one end of the house. The porch was often lavished with as many as three or four exterior colors, and an abundance of gingerbread trim provided an eye-catching blend of materials and patterns. Proper Victorians often enjoyed breakfast, luncheon, tea, and evening visits on these grand porches, and as a result, the porch became a parlor of sorts during the summer.

The same could be said of the summer homes owned by the well-to-do—the center of activity was indeed the porch. Whether at the shore or in a summer colony, the porch was outfitted with casual wicker furnishings and perhaps a hammock or two. While tea was a daily ritual when summering away from the city home, women also gathered on the porch during the day to enjoy finger sandwiches, cookies, lemonade, and light conversation.

More remote retreats, such as the late-nineteenth-century "camps" that sprang up in the Adirondack Mountains, were typically outfitted with rustic furniture, and the porch was no exception. Massive wooden chairs, tables, settees, and so on crafted from tree branches, twigs, bark, and roots predominated on the porch and became so popular that it wasn't long before several companies began mass-producing rustic furnishings to fill the growing demand.

Above: The quintessential front porch combines color and pattern in the form of gingerbread trim. A hanging basket and flower box contribute soft accents and salute the Victorian love of nature.

Right: This peaceful porch is outfitted with the same care as the rest of the house. Special comforts include a hammock for lazy afternoon rest and relaxation. True Victorian spirit pervades, not only in furnishings and accessories, but in architectural details as well. The stenciled ceiling, the porch columns, the tiled floor, and the exposed rock wall all combine to establish a backdrop that is in itself highly decorative.

With changing architectural styles after the dawn of the twentieth century, noise from automobiles, and the development of suburbs, the front porch was gradually replaced by the backyard patio with its privacy from the street and neighbors. Fortunately, front porches are today experiencing renewed popularity as historic homes are rescued, urban neighborhoods are revitalized, and new homes are constructed with nineteenth-century style.

Creating a Victorian Porch

You don't have to own a nineteenth-century home or build a Victorian Revival–style house to enjoy a porch and outfit it in typical Victorian fashion. Many homes have small porches or backyard decks that can be made comfortable and inviting by borrowing ideas from the past. Comfort, natural beauty, and no-fuss furnishings and accessories are the keys to enjoying the splendor of the old-fashioned porch.

The porch or veranda offers visitors a first impression of your home. Victorians were inclined to believe that this meeting point—where indoors and outdoors join as one—should blend with the natural surroundings and showcase the home's palette. It was common practice during the later Victorian era to paint the porch ceiling light blue in imitation of the sky, and floors, painted to protect them from the weather, were usually white, gray, or green. These ideas still work well today.

The porch itself was painted according to the color or colors chosen for the house, and several colors may have been used on a very ornate porch to define all sorts of fretwork.

Many of today's homes feature a fully enclosed porch or sunroom, which is perfectly suited to decoration in the Victorian style. These rooms have the feel of a porch with the advantages of year-round use and protection from the weather.

FURNISHINGS

After you've determined that your porch is structurally sound, made any necessary repairs, and painted it according to the style and color of your home, thoughts naturally turn to furnishing this extended living space.

Wicker—a catchall word used to describe furniture crafted from rattan, reed, willow, cane, and later paper fiber—has long been popular for outdoor use and began appearing on the Victorian porch during the 1800s. Early wicker pieces were constructed with hardwood frames that made them sturdy, and their natural materials proved to be weather resistant. While much of the wicker produced later in the nineteenth century was quite ornate, by the turn of the century the emphasis on cleanliness and sanitary measures throughout the house made simple open-weave or latticework designs

A romantic dark wicker chair and settee are playfully treated to rugged, rustic-looking plaid cushions for a casual, outdoorsy effect. By adding select accessories—a cutting basket, a lantern, and a footstool—the perfect room in the woods has been created.

pieces included rockers, chairs, settees, small tables, and planters. Three-piece porch sets were popular, and generally included a chair, rocker, and settee. While some wicker furnishings were left natural and simply coated with varnish, porch pieces were usually painted white or green.

Wicker is ideally suited to the covered porch, where furniture can be somewhat protected. Open spaces—such as a deck or patio—are better served by wooden furnishings with a water-repellent treatment.

If antique wicker furnishings are your passion, inspect individual pieces carefully to determine that they are in good condition and of sound construction. Chairs, tables, plant stands, and rockers are still easy to locate by visiting antiques shops, shows, and estate sales. In addition, there are dealers across the country that specialize in vintage wicker—refer to the source directory.

If you decide to invest in reproduction wicker, quality is imperative. Keep in mind that a hardwood frame will guarantee that your furniture will last for years, and pieces constructed with nails are better than those held together with staples.

Other furnishings at home on the porch or the open-air deck include slat-back wooden chairs and settees, wooden rockers, porch swings (which can be hung from the ceiling on a porch or used on a deck in a free-standing form), or Adirondack-style chairs.

Rustic furnishings, long associated with mountain retreats, are ideal in a country setting or in an eclectic mix of outdoor pieces. Displaying both the glory of nature and the talent of the artisans who crafted them, rustic pieces of twig furniture from hickory, ash, elm, spruce, birch, cedar, or willow appealed to the Victorians' desire to escape back to the woods in a rapidly industrializing society.

popular indoors as well as on the porch. While much of this porch furniture is collectively referred to as "Bar Harbor" wicker (named after the resort in Maine), there were variations. Other styles were also named after vacation spots where grand hotels furnished massive porches with versatile wicker. For example, actual Bar Harbor wicker pieces were constructed from thick reeds, and chairs featured square backs, flat arms, and an open-weave, crisscross design.

Newport or Southampton wicker chairs were constructed with romantic heart-shaped backs or curved backs, while Cape Cod wicker was created from tightly woven reed.

Mission-style wicker (which came about as a result of the Arts and Crafts Movement) had a closed-weave design and a more mas-

This picture-perfect setting includes a cozy table and wicker chairs for lunch or tea. A wonderfully ornate wicker rocker stands by for simply enjoying a quiet moment or taking in a quiet summer afternoon. Porch rockers are synonymous with comfort and relaxation.

culine form. This style was being made by 1900 and turned up on the front porch as well as inside the house.

A variety of wicker furnishings could be purchased from department stores or mail-order catalogs to outfit the porch. Popular

As early as the 1840s, twig furnishings were being crafted in a Gothic style for use in the garden. Chairs, benches, and planters created from roots and twigs were the perfect touch in romantic gardens gone natural with a profusion of flowers and greenery.

"Gypsy" furnishings (so called because they were often crafted by bands of gypsies) made of willow featured loop-backs on chairs, and Appalachian twig furniture, made of hickory or willow during the late 1800s and early 1900s, are often recognizable by the bentwood design featured on chairs.

While rustic furniture is often generally referred to as Adirondack style, the form most closely identified with this upper New York State mountain region is the wooden slat-back chair with wide arms called an Adirondack chair. This region is also noted for stunning creations made of bark and twigs; especially notable are the geometric designs and mosaics on larger camp furnishings, such as beds, settees, and sideboards.

Before the turn of the century, the Old Hickory Chair Company of Martinsville, Indiana, was turning out rustic furniture to fill the demand for such items in camps, resorts, and parks across the country. Popular pieces for outdoor use included the usual assortment of chairs, rockers, settees, tables, porch swings, planters, and benches.

Rustic furniture has received a great deal of attention in the past several years and is now considered by many to be a form of American folk art. Antique pieces are available but prices have been steadily rising. Examine vintage examples carefully to determine if there is any insect damage or rot.

New rustic furnishings are available as a growing number of artisans turn their attention—and their talent—to handcrafting wooden furnishings.

The country porch or the backyard deck or patio are both well suited to these pieces, which echo the Victorian love of nature.

DECORATIVE ACCESSORIES

The Victorians celebrated nature and brought its beauty up onto the porch to be enjoyed. They took full advantage of wicker planters, clay pots, decorative urns, and double- or triple-tiered wire plant stands to decorate the porch with an abundance of flowers. They also used woven baskets, wooden boxes, wireware baskets, and so on to hang lush greenery, trailing vines, and colorful floral arrangements from the porch for passersby to enjoy and to enhance the beauty of the porch.

All these ideas are as practical today as they were a hundred years ago and are the ideal way to decorate the porch or other outdoor areas. Vintage or reproduction planters are available in a variety of styles and mate-

Above: This homey, Victorian-inspired porch is beautifully furnished with wooden pieces that have been given a refreshing coat of white paint. The cushioned settee and armchair are accompanied by—what else?—a comfy rocker.

Left: Decorative accessories define this eye-catching sunporch. A vintage chaise longue with a comfy cushion is accompanied by an ornate wireware planter filled to overflowing with summer blooms. Creative use of a trellis allows climbing vines to adorn the wall.

rials, and the consensus seems to be the more the merrier—you can never have too many plants or flowers.

Dress furnishings with comfy, floral cushions and pillows, and drape a lace scarf over a small tabletop. Sisal matting or a colorful throw rug or two can be used on the porch for a soft touch underfoot, and bam-

Above: Combining all the pleasing elements of casual Victorian design, this enclosed porch blends cushioned wicker furnishings with a no-fuss sisal matting for a soft touch underfoot. Note also that color and texture are enhanced with the addition of light-controlling shades.

Left: This casual porch setting is given a goodly dose of color by accessorizing the chairs with brightly patterned cushions. A cheerful area rug and an abundance of flowers add harmonizing color, pattern, and texture.

boo shades (or matchstick blinds) can be hung on the porch to filter sunlight.

If you don't have a porch or deck, don't give up on the idea of bringing Victorian spirit to an outdoor setting. Look to your yard, a small garden, or even a terrace as a special place of quiet relaxation or retreat. Subtle Victorian style can be added to a small space with a strategically placed chair or bench in the nineteenth-century style. If you have the advantage of space, a small gazebo or an arbor complete with a bench can provide the perfect quiet spot for an intimate conversation or a peaceful afternoon with a good book. Use your imagination and you're sure to find the possibilities are limitless. Above all, enjoy your outdoor space and savor the beauty and wonder of it all—just as the Victorians did.

Glossary of Victorian Terms

a la Russe   a style of dining in which the food is placed on the sideboard rather than the table, with the servants carving the meat, thus freeing the host from this task.

American Empire   a furniture style inspired by Grecian forms, popular in America from the 1820s through the 1840s. American Empire furniture displays rectangular shapes, and was constructed of cherry or mahogany and adorned with gilt stenciling, paw feet, marble tops, and delicate carvings. The sleigh bed and center table were products of American Empire style.

Anaglypta   an embossed wallcovering developed during the nineteenth century from paper fibers. Anaglypta is being reproduced today.

antimacassar   a crocheted doily placed on chairs to protect delicate fabrics from the hair oils commonly used by men during the nineteenth century.

art glass   the stained glass used to create artistic windows in late-nineteenth-century Victorian homes or used in the making of lampshades during the 1890s.

ashlar wallpaper   a wallpaper that had the look of cut stone. Ashlar wallpaper was especially popular in the 1840s and 1850s.

Bohemian glass   clear and colored glassware in shades of amber, red, cobalt, and amethyst, often with engraved patterns such as florals, animals, and birds.

brocade   a rich fabric with a raised pattern, usually in muted colors and sometimes incorporating metallics.

Brussels   a looped-pile tapestry carpet that was extremely popular during the nineteenth century.

carnival glass   mass-produced iridescent glass, appearing shortly after the turn of the century, imitating the costlier iridescent glass produced by designers such as Louis Tiffany.

ceiling medallion   a decorative disklike element made of wood or plaster used to adorn the ceilings in the Victorian home. Ceiling medallions were considered quite formal and were therefore generally reserved for the parlor and dining room.

chair rail   a molded wooden strip used around the perimeter of a room to protect walls from being marked by the back of chairs.

chintz   a printed cotton fabric with a glossy look, popular in both the parlor and the bedroom for use as curtains, pillows, and upholstery.

coffered ceiling   a decorative ceiling featuring recessed panels.

cornice   the projecting horizontal trim at the top of a wall or other architectural feature.

color theory   a term in interior design referring to the principles behind selecting and matching colors. Color theory was widely discussed in magazines by the 1850s, and women were advised to paint rooms in either harmonizing or contrasting colors.

cottage furniture   machine-made softwood furnishings (1840–1900) that were painted in light or pastel shades such as pink, lavender, gray, or blue and then hand-decorated with floral designs, imitative graining, or stenciling. Cottage furniture was especially popular in the bedroom.

cretonne   a type of durable cotton or linen commonly used for curtains.

dado   the bottom portion of an interior wall, usually used in the context of the tripartite wall treatment favored by Victorians.

damask   a soft, flat-patterned fabric woven on jacquard looms.

drugget   a floor covering made of coarse wool cloth or wool and flax. A drugget was used atop wood floors or to protect costly rugs.

dry sink   a basin of soapstone, iron, or granite cased in a low wooden cupboard with storage space below the sink. Water from a well or a holding tank could be pumped into the dry sink.

Eastlake furniture   handcrafted or factory-made rectangular furnishings (1870–1890s) made of cherry, walnut, oak, ash, or chestnut and embellished with incised lines or carved, geometric patterns. The style was named after Charles Eastlake, design reformer and author of the landmark book *Hints on Household Taste*.

electrolier   a hanging electric light fixture, which replaced the gasolier and the chandelier; gasoliers were sometimes converted into electroliers.

epergne   a tiered glass or metalwork centerpiece, which could hold candles, flowers in vases, and/or dishes.

étagère   a tall, elaborate stand or corner stand for displaying bric-a-brac, keepsakes, and so on. The étagère was often the most ornamental furnishing in the Victorian parlor.

field   the middle expanse of an interior wall in the tripartite wall scheme.

flocked wallpaper   a wallpaper with a raised texture, imitating damask fabric; also referred to as velvet paper.

Flow Blue   a popular blue transfer print used on ironstone.

fresco papers   decorative wallpapers with landscape scenes or floral motifs that made the wall appear to be painted panels.

frieze   a decorative band around the perimeter of a wall, usually achieved with wallpaper, though also with stenciling; part of the tripartite wall. Also, a dense, cut-pile carpeting with a nubby look.

gasolier   a hanging light fixture fueled by gas, often adorned with glass globes, prisms, or other decoration.

glass curtain   an undercurtain made of lace or muslin used when dressing a window in layers.

Gothic Revival   a furniture style popular from 1840 to 1860. The romance of the middle ages and the subtle influence of the architectural features of French cathedrals combined in these predominantly rosewood or oak furnishings to produce chairs, settees, etc. with Gothic arches, carved trefoils, and delicate spool turnings. Gothic Revival may also refer to architectural style.

graniteware   kitchenware of enamel-covered cast iron, and later sheet steel, popular in the late 1800s and early 1900s. Its speckled, mottled, or swirled designs were most often produced in gray, brown, blue, and red in the United States, and iris, terra-cotta, brown-black, and white in Europe. European pieces were often adorned with attractive hand-painted or stenciled floral or nature motifs.

hairwork   detailed artwork crafted from human hair, very popular in Victorian times.

High Style   a fashion, design, or style at its fullest flower.

Hoosier cabinet   a piece of kitchen furniture that featured cupboards and drawers for storage, a work surface for food preparation, and often a flour bin, a ventilated metal bread drawer, or a spice shelf hidden by tambour doors.

ingrain carpet   a flat, woven carpet in which narrow strips are sewn together to create the floor covering. Ingrain carpets were quite popular since they were reversible.

ironstone   a type of durable white dishware, which middle-class Victorians found an affordable alternative to fine china.

Italianate   a highly romantic architectural style popular in the 1860s. Italianate villas were generally square in shape with two or three stories, bracketed eaves, arched windows, cupolas, and a full front porch, and were often painted in earth tones.

jabot   a fall of fabric cascading from a valance or a swag.

Japanesque   a style of decorating that incorporated Oriental motifs, which lent an exotic air to the room and reflected the Victorian love of travel.

lambrequin   an elaborate and decorative fabric valance adorned with tassels, fringe, etc. used in opulent window dressings.

library lamp   a kerosene hanging lamp with a brass body and a painted shade.

Lincrusta   an embossed wall covering first introduced in 1877, created from linseed oil and a canvas-backed paper. Lincrusta was a popular dado treatment on Victorian-era walls, and is enjoying renewed interest today.

majolica   pottery with high-relief decorations and a clear lead glaze, which was imported from England and France, and produced by a number of American firms as well. Designs were inspired by nature, with flowers, leaves, fruit, shells, birds, and fish covering the surfaces of plates, pitchers, teapots, jardinieres, and other such objects.

Mission   a style of oak furniture that features sturdy, straight lines with leather or canvas upholstery. Simplicity combined with beauty and utility is the essence of Mission-style furniture; also referred to as Arts and

Crafts furniture, as the Mission style grew out of the Arts and Crafts Movement.

molding　a decorative strip used as an architectural ornament.

oilcloth　a floor covering created by preparing a sturdy cloth with paint and varnish. Oilcloths were especially popular in the kitchen before linoleum was introduced; also called floorcloth.

piazza　a covered gallery, extending from either side of the front entrance, common in Gothic Revival–style homes.

pie safe　an enclosed cupboard with doors of wire mesh or punched tin, which allowed air to circulate around baked goods.

plate rail　narrow shelving running along the upper portion of a wall, used to display plates or other objects.

portico　a covered walkway with massive columns found at the entrance to a building. The portico is especially common in the Greek Revival style.

portiere　a fabric doorway curtain used between rooms (such as the front parlor and sitting room) to block drafts and as a decorative element.

pyrography　a decorative art in which designs are burned into wood, used to adorn plaques, boxes, etc.

Renaissance Revival　a furniture style usually crafted from walnut (1860s–1880s). These pieces are easily recognized by their massive size, angular shapes, and carved or applied ornaments such as medallions, pediments, and scrolls. The architectural style of this period is also referred to as Renaissance Revival.

Rococo Revival　revival-style furniture with French influence in which rosewood or black walnut pieces (1850s–1870s) featured serpentine backs on sofas and carved fruits, flowers, etc. on other pieces. Also, Rococo Revival refers to the architectural style associated with this French influence.

slag glass　a form of art glass that appeared quite often in furnishings (for example, cupboard doors) during the late nineteenth and early twentieth centuries. Slag glass, milky or cloudy in appearance, was often created in amber, green, or white colors.

student's lamp　a kerosene lamp often used on a desk because its cantilever form, in which the stem connecting the lamp and the fuel source were adjacent to each other, allowed light to be cast directly over papers on the desktop without the body of the lamp being in the way.

transfer print　a design applied by means of a multi-step process. First, a copper plate bearing the pattern was coated with a cobalt pigment, and tissue paper was laid over the design. This was placed on plates or other dishes to "transfer" the design to the object, and then the piece was fired.

trefoil　an ornament with a stylized, three-leafed shape similar to that of a clover.

tripartite　a type of wall treatment popular from the 1870s through the early 1890s in which a wall was divided into three horizontal sections: the dado or wainscoting on the bottom; a "field" or expanse in the middle, which was painted or papered; and a wallpaper frieze at the top.

Turkish chair　a large, overstuffed, tufted chair upholstered in plush, multi-tone velours and ornamented with decorative tasseled fringe. These furnishings (couches as well as chairs) were in vogue during the late nineteenth century when the Victorian fascination with the Far East and Turkish or Moorish cultures resulted in the creation of "Turkish corners" in many parlors and sitting rooms.

Venetian curtain　a type of curtain, now known as a balloon curtain, popular during the 1890s.

Victorian　referring to a period of time during the nineteenth century (1837–1901) when Queen Victoria of England ruled as sovereign; also the styles and attitudes that prevailed during this era.

wainscot　wood paneling used to cover the lower area of an interior wall.

Wilton　a cut-pile velvet carpet popular during the nineteenth century.

yellowware　pottery that took on a yellowish cast once it was fired. Later in the nineteenth century it was decorated with white, brown, green, or blue bands, or washed in a Rockingham glaze, which gave the pieces a mottled brown look. By the end of the century, molded floral designs and incised lines were also being applied. Common items included nesting bowls, rolling pins, teapots, molds, and pitchers.

Chronology of Victorian Furniture Styles and Trends in Interior Design

1830s

American Empire–style furnishings, with their rectangular shapes, gilt stenciling, paw feet, and delicate carvings, were in vogue and remained popular through the 1840s.

In 1837 Queen Victoria of England took the throne and reigned until 1901—hence the "Victorian" era.

Interior design found walls being covered with light shades of hand-mixed paints or costly European wallpapers.

Floors were painted or covered with simple matting or floorcloths.

1840s

Gothic Revival–style furnishings were introduced and handcrafted or machine-made through the 1860s. Gothic Revival featured carved trefoils, pointed arches, and spool turnings in oak or rosewood.

Factory-made cottage furniture with spool turnings and/or pastel painted finishes proved a popular alternative to more costly styles and was produced through the end of the century.

Affordable machine-made wallpapers were introduced with common patterns including landscape scenes, striped papers, velvet papers, and historical scenes.

Windows were routinely outfitted with shutters, fabric blinds, venetian blinds, or simple curtains.

1850s

Rococo Revival–style furnishings made their debut and remained quite fashionable through the 1870s. Designs were French-inspired, and featured serpentine sofa backs and carved fruits, flowers, etc., crafted mainly of rosewood and black walnut.

Cast-iron furniture and accessories for the home and garden were being manufactured with the same delicate forms and embellishments identified on Rococo Revival–style pieces.

The introduction of color theory found interior design focusing on rooms decorated with either harmonizing or contrasting color schemes.

Carpeting became widely available and was considered not only a decorative element but a necessity in most homes.

Window dressings became more elaborate with layers including a shade, an undercurtain, ornate draperies, and a valance.

1860s

Renaissance Revival–style furnishings, with their angular shapes, medallions and scrolls, and massive size, were in vogue between the 1860s and 1880s.

Purchasing furniture in suites that included several matching pieces became commonplace. Parlor suites including a sofa or settee, a lady's chair, and side chairs were especially popular.

Window treatments became even more excessive and opulent with the addition of lambrequins.

Wall-to-wall carpeting with large floral or geometric designs was found in most homes by this time.

1870s

Charles Eastlake's book, *Hints on Household Taste*, became available in America and influenced both interior design and furniture design for the next two decades.

Eastlake-style furnishings were popular between the 1870s and early 1890s. Furniture in the Eastlake style reflected the reforms the designer advocated, and featured incised lines and geometric patterns in cherry, walnut, oak, ash, or chestnut.

"Japanesque" designs and decorating with exotic accessories became fashionable, hinting at worldliness, travel, and an appreciation of other cultures. This trend lasted through the end of the nineteenth century.

Exposed hardwood or parquet floors with Oriental rugs replaced wall-to-wall carpets.

The tripartite wall treatment in interior design became the rage—a trend that lasted until the early 1890s, when simplified wall treatments were called for. Popular colors included olive, plum, claret, terra-cotta, citron, and peacock blue.

1880s

The Aesthetic Movement introduced nature-inspired furnishings in bamboo and wicker, as well as decorative elements such as peacock feathers, to interior design.

Mail-order furnishings such as the popular golden oak and factory-produced Eastlake style pieces made the latest fashions available to even remote areas across the country.

While ornate window treatments and Oriental rugs remained in vogue, the tripartite wall treatment reached new heights of popularity via the use of corresponding wallpapers to create a dado, fill, and frieze.

1890s

Art Nouveau designs in wallpaper, glassware, etc. featured romantic floral motifs, swirls, and flowing curves.

The Arts and Crafts Movement introduced angular Mission furniture and called for simplification in interior design.

As the tripartite wall treatment fell out of favor it was replaced by a two-part wall treatment featuring painted or papered walls with a simple frieze. Muted shades of green, earth tones, and gray-blue became popular color choices.

Window treatments became less fussy with simple rod-pocket panels of lace or muslin turning up in many middle-class homes.

Although Colonial Revival–style furnishings made their debut with the 1876 Centennial celebrations, they were especially popular around the turn of the century.

Source Directory

This source directory has been compiled with the do-it-yourself approach in mind. All products are available at the retail level or can be purchased via mail order. Everything you need to create a Victorian home is at your fingertips, whether it's a source for reproduction wall coverings, carpets or flooring, ceiling decorations, antique or reproduction light fixtures, window dressings, antique or reproduction furniture, select Victorian accessories, or treasured antiques and collectibles.

WALL TREATMENTS

Bradbury & Bradbury—P.O. Box 155, Benicia, CA 94510; Telephone: (707) 746-1900.
Studio specializing in reproduction nineteenth-century wallpapers. Patterns available to create an authentic tripartite wall treatment with dado, field, and frieze. Call or write for information regarding catalog.

Carol Mead Design—RR#3, Box 3396, West Addison, VT 05491; Telephone: (802) 759-2692.
Specializes in hand-printed reproduction Victorian and Arts and Crafts wallpapers. Call or write for information regarding catalog.

Crown Corporation NA—1801 Wynkoop Street, Suite 235, Denver, CO 80202-1067; Telephone: (800) 422-2099.
Specializes in Lincrusta and Anaglypta embossed wallcoverings. Write for a free catalog.

Designs in Tile—P.O. Box 358, Mount Shasta, CA 96067; Telephone: (916) 926-2629.
Studio specializing in Victorian hand-decorated tiles. Call or write for information regarding brochure.

Eisenhart Wallcovering—1649 Broadway, Hanover, PA 17331; Telephone: (800) 726-3267.
Specializes in Victorian wallpapers featuring florals, foliage, architectural patterns, and designs imitating stone or marble. Call or write for information on sample book.

Fuller O'Brien Paints—2001 W. Washington Ave., P.O. Box 17, South Bend, IN 46624; Telephone: (800) 338-8084.
Has a line of re-created nineteenth-century paint colors for both interior and exterior use. Call or write for information on color samples.

Mt. Diablo Handprints Inc.—P.O. Box 726, Benicia, CA 94510; Telephone: (707) 745-3388.
Specializes in reproduction historical wallcoverings. Call or write for information regarding catalog.

Richard E. Thibaut Inc.—480 Frelinghuysen Avenue, Newark, NJ 07114; Telephone: (800) 223-0704.
Specializes in Victorian wallcoverings and fabrics. Call or write for brochure.

FLOORING

American Olean Tile Company—Design Dept., Olean, NY; Telephone: (716) 372-4300.
Specializes in tiles for flooring as well as wall treatments, including small squares and hexagons in unglazed ceramic mosaics. Available at retail flooring and carpet centers.

Armstrong—Telephone: (800) 233-3823.
Extensive selection of resilient vinyl flooring. Call for location of nearest retailer.

Clair Murray—P.O. Box 390, Ascutney, VT 05030; Telephone: (800) 252-4733.
Specializes in hand-hooked rugs and kits, needlepoint, and quilts. Call or write for information on the Finished Home Accessory Catalog (or call 1-800-345-KITS for the Claire Murray Kit Catalog).

Family Heirloom Weavers—775 Meadow View Drive, Red Lion, PA 17356; Telephone: (717) 246-2431.
Specializes in reproduction ingrain carpets. Call or write for information regarding brochure.

Historic Floors of Oshkosh—P.O. Box 572, Oshkosh, WI 54902; Telephone: (414) 233-5066.
Specializes in reproduction wood flooring, borders, and parquets created from oak, cherry, maple, or walnut woods. Call or write for information.

J.R. Burrows & Co.—P.O. Box 522, Rockland, MA 02370; Telephone: (617) 982-1812.
Specializes in reproduction Brussels and Wilton carpets and also offers Victorian wallpapers, fabrics, lace curtains, etc. Call or write for information regarding catalog.

Kentucky Wood Floors—P.O. Box 33276, Louisville, KY 40232; Telephone: (502) 451-6024.
Specializes in hardwood flooring, parquet, decorative borders. Call or write for information on brochure.

CEILINGS

AA Abbingdon Affiliates Inc.—2149 Utica Avenue, Brooklyn, NY 11234; Telephone: (718) 258-8333.
Specializes in Victorian tin ceilings and also offers ceiling medallions. Call or write for information on brochure.

Chelsea Decorative Metal Co.—9603 Moonlight Drive, Houston, TX 77096; Telephone: (713) 721-9200.
Specializes in pressed-tin ceilings. Call or write for information on brochure.

Classic Ceilings—902 East Commonwealth Avenue, Fullerton, CA 92631-4518; Telephone: (800) 992-8700.
Specializes in tin ceilings as well as Anaglypta embossed wallcoverings and ceiling medallions. Call or write regarding catalog.

Cumberland Woodcraft Co., Inc.—P.O. Drawer 609, Carlise, PA 17013; Telephone: (717) 243-0063.
Specializes in Victorian ceiling treatments as well as wainscoting for walls and assorted fretwork. Call or write for information on brochure.

J.P. Weaver Co.—941 Air Way, Glendale, CA 91201; Telephone: (818) 841-5700.
Specializes in ornaments for the decoration of ceilings, wall, mantels, doors, and furniture. Call or write for information on design brochure.

W.F. Norman Corp.—P.O. Box 323, 214 North Cedar Street, Nevada, MO 64772-0323; Telephone: (800) 641-4038.
Specializes in tin ceilings. Call or write for information regarding catalog.

Yowler & Shepps—3529 Main Street, Conestoga, PA 17516; Telephone: (717) 872-2820.
Specializes in stencils for Victorian wall or ceiling decoration. Call or write for information regarding catalog.

LIGHTING

Fantasy Lighting Inc.—7126 Melrose Avenue, Los Angeles, CA 90046; Telephone: (213) 933-7244.
Specializes in Victorian glass lamps and fabric shades with decorative fringe or beadwork. Call or write for information regarding brochure.

Gaslight Time—823 President Street,
Brooklyn, NY 11215; Telephone: (718)
789-7185.
*Offers a selection of restored antique fixtures and
table or floor lamps. Call or write for information regarding catalog.*

Historic Lighting Restoration—10341
Jewell Lake Court, Fenton, MI 48430;
Telephone: (313) 629-4934.
*Large selection of vintage gas and electric fixtures,
reproduction (electrified) kerosene chandeliers,
and restoration services available. Call or
write for information regarding catalog.*

Lamp Glass—P.O. Box 791, Cambridge,
MA 02140; Telephone: (617) 497-0770.
*Specializes in replacement glass shades for a vari-
ety of lamps including student lamps, bankers
lamps, hurricane lamps, etc. Call or write for
information regarding brochure.*

New England Stained Glass Studios—
5 Center Street, P.O. Box 381, West
Stockbridge, MA 01266; Telephone:
(413) 232-7181.
Specializes in reproduction Tiffany lamps.

Roy Electric—1054 Coney Island Avenue,
Brooklyn, NY 11230; Telephone: (800)
366-3347.
*Specializes in antique and reproduction Victorian
lighting fixtures and lamps. Call or write for
information regarding catalog.*

Stanely Galleries—2118 North Clark Street,
Chicago, IL 60614; Telephone: (312)
281-1614.
*Specializes in antique (Victorian and early-
twentieth-century) lighting fixtures and
lamps as well as furnishings.*

Yestershades—4327 Hawthorne, Portland,
OR 97214; Telephone: (503) 235-5647.
*Specializes in reproduction Victorian lampshades
created with satin, silk, lace, decorative fringe,
etc. Call or write regarding catalog.*

WINDOW TREATMENTS

Country Curtains Inc.—Red Lion Inn,
Dept. 1933, Stockbridge, MA 01262;
Telephone: (800) 876-6123.
*Large selection of curtains in a variety of styles
and fabrics including lace. Call or write for
free catalog.*

Goodman Fabrications—P.O. Box 8164;
Prairie Village, KS 66208; Telephone:
(816) 942-0832.
*Specializes in wood blinds, roller shades, and cus-
tomized window treatments. Call or write for
information.*

Heritage Imports, Inc.—309 South Street,
Box 328, Pella, IA 50219; Telephone:
(800) 354-0668.
*Specializes in lace curtains and accessories. Call or
write for free brochure.*

Linen & Lace—4 Lafayette Street,
Washington, MO 63090; Telephone:
(314) 239-6499.
*Specializes in imported Scottish lace curtains and
accessories. Call or write for free catalog.*

London Lace—167 Newbury Street,
Boston, MA 02116; Telephone: (617)
267-3506.
*Specializes in lace panels and yardage imported
from Scotland. Call or write for information
regarding catalog.*

Shutter Depot—Route 2, Box 157,
Greenville, GA 30222; Telephone: (706)
672-1214.
*Specializes in interior and exterior shutters, cus-
tom finished or unfinished. Call or write for
brochure.*

Vintage Valances—P.O. Box 43326,
Cincinnati, OH 45243; Telephone: (513)
561-8665.
*Specializes in custom-made drapes of historical
design.*

FURNISHINGS—ANTIQUE

Antiquarian Traders—4851 Alameda Street,
Los Angeles, CA 90058; Telephone:
(213) 687-4000.
*Specializes in Victorian furnishings and vintage
lighting fixtures. Call or write for information
regarding catalog.*

Dovetail Antiques—474 White Pine Road,
Columbus, NJ 08022; Telephone: (609)
298-5245.
*Specializes in authentic vintage wicker furniture
circa 1880–1930. Call or write for information
regarding catalog.*

Farm River Antiques—26 Broadway,
North Haven, CT 06473; Telephone:
(203) 239-2434.
*Specializes in antique nineteenth-century
furniture.*

Joan Bogart—1392 Old Northern
Boulevard, Roslyn, NY 11576;
Telephone: (516) 621-2454.
*Specializes in High Style Victorian antique furni-
ture and accessories. Call or write for informa-
tion regarding video or merchandise.*

Prince Alberts Victorian Furnishings—431 Thames Street, Newport, RI 02340; Telephone: (401) 848-5372.

Specializes in antique Victorian furniture for the parlor, bedroom, and dining room. Call or write for free brochure.

Ralph Kylloe—298 High Range, Londonderry, NH 03053; Telephone: (603) 437-2920.

Specializes in antique rustic furnishings and accessories.

Southampton Antiques—172 College Highway, Route 10, Southampton, MA 01073; Telephone: (413) 527-1022.

Specializes in antique American oak and Victorian furniture. Call or write for information on custom-made videos.

Urban Artifacts—4700 Wissahickon Avenue, Philadelphia, PA 19144; Telephone: (800) 621-1962.

Stocks a wide selection of Victorian oak, mahogany, and walnut furniture as well as antique fireplace mantels.

FURNISHINGS— REPRODUCTIONS

Brass Bed Shoppe—12421 Cedar Road, Cleveland, OH 44106; Telephone: (216) 229-4900.

Specializes in brass and iron beds. Call or write for free catalog.

Heirloom Reproduction—1 834 West 5th Street, Montgomery, AL 36106; Telephone: (800) 288-1513.

Specializes in reproduction Victorian furniture with an extensive selection of fabrics. Call or write for information regarding catalog.

Hope & Wilder Home—454 Broome Street, New York, NY 10013; Telephone: (212) 966-9010.

Specializes in home furnishings, including iron beds, slipcovers, custom upholstery, and a wide selection of fabrics.

L. & J.G. Stickley Inc.—P.O. Box 480, Manlius, NY 13104-0480; Telephone: (315) 682-5500.

Specializes in reproduction Arts and Crafts–inspired Mission-style furnishings.

Lexington Furniture—P.O. Box 1008, Lexington, NC 27293-1008; Telephone: (800) 544-4694.

Produces a line of oak reproduction furnishings for the Victorian bedroom. Call or write for catalog information.

Magnolia Hall—725 Andover Drive, Atlanta, GA 30327; Telephone: (404) 237-9725.

Specializes in reproduction Victorian furnishings for every room in the house. Call or write regarding catalog.

Martha M. House Furniture—1022 South Decatur Street, Montgomery, AL 36104; Telephone: (205) 264-3558.

Specializes in reproduction Victorian furnishings and French furnishings crafted from solid mahogany, many featuring Italian marble tops. Call or write for catalog information.

Wicker Warehouse—195 South River Street, Hackensack, NJ 07601; Telephone: (201) 342-6709.

Specializes in American-manufactured wicker as well as imports for any room in the house. Call or write for catalog information.

FURNISHINGS— KITCHEN AND BATH

Antique Baths & Kitchens—2220 Carloton Way, Santa Barbara, CA 93109; Telephone: (805) 962-8598.

Specializes in pedestal sinks and pull-chain toilets for the bath, as well as copper and brass kitchen sinks and assorted hardware. Call or write regarding catalog.

The Fixture Exchange—P.O. Box 307, Bainbridge, GA 31717; Telephone: (912) 246-4938.

Everything you need for the Victorian-inspired bath, including claw-foot tubs, pedestal sinks, etc. Call or write regarding catalog.

The Kennebec Company—1 Front Street, Bath, ME 04530; Telephone: (207) 443-2131.

Specializes in custom cabinetry designs for the kitchen. Call or write for catalog information.

Northern Refrigerator Company—21149 Northland Drive, P.O. Box 204, Paris, MI 49307.

Specializes in reproduction "icebox" style refrigerators for an authentic look in the Victorian kitchen. Write for information regarding product packet.

Renovators' Supply—Renovators Old Mill, Dept. 9565, Miller Falls, MA 01349; Telephone: (800) 659-2211.

Specializes in Victorian bathroom furnishings and accessories, decorative hardware, lighting fixtures, and vintage wall treatments. Call or write for free catalog.

Wellborn Cabinet, Inc.—P.O. Box 1210, Route 1, Highway 77S, Ashland, AL 36251; Telephone: (800) 336-8040.

Specializes in custom cabinetry created in oak, hickory, maple, or cherry. Call or write regarding brochure.

FURNISHINGS—PORCH AND GARDEN

Adirondack Store & Gallery—109 Saranac Avenue, Lake Placid, NY 12946; Telephone: (518) 523-2646.
Specializes in hickory and birch-bark furnishings as well as rustic accessories.

Barlow Tyrie Inc.—1263 Glen Avenue, Suite 230, Moorestown, NJ 08057; Telephone: (800) 451-7467.
Specializes in reproduction cast-aluminum Victorian garden furniture and teakwood furniture. Call or write for free brochure.

Lloyd/Flanders Industries—3010 10th Street, P.O. Box 550, Menominee, MI 49858; Telephone: (906) 863-4491.
Specializes in weatherized wicker furnishings ideal for use on the porch. Call or write for free brochure.

Victorian Attic—P.O. Box 831, Main Road, Mattituc, NY 11952; Telephone: (516) 298-4789.
Specializes in reproduction Victorian garden furniture created of cast metal as well as an extensive line of garden and porch accessories. Call or write regarding catalog.

Walter J. Bass Co.—1432 West Grand River, Box 397, Williamston, MI 48895.
Specializes in cedar gazebo kits. Call or write for free catalog.

DECORATIVE ACCESSORIES AND COLLECTIBLES

Bep's Antiques—2051 Magazine Street, New Orleans, LA 70115; Telephone: (504) 525-7726.
Specializes in antiques, including Dutch and English tiles, that can be used in a number of decorative ways throughout the Victorian home.

Beverly Bremer Silver Shop—3164 Peachtree Road, NE, Atlanta, GA 30305; Telephone: (404) 261-4009.
Specializes in sterling flatware, collectibles, and decorative antiques for the home.

The Chuctanunda Antique Co.—One 4th Avenue, Amsterdam, NY 12010; Telephone: (518) 843-3983.
Specializes in antique French and European enamel ware for the kitchen and bath. Call or write for free brochure and antiques show schedule. Does a large mail-order business.

Cox Studios—1004 South 9th Street, Cannon City, CO 81212; Telephone: (719) 429-1457.
Specializes in stained glass and etched glass designs as well as firescreens, decorative boxes, etc. Call or write for information.

Delights of a Queen—40 South Main Street, South Deerfield, MA 01373; Telephone: (413) 665-3511.
Specializes in Victorian home accessories such as plush pillows, tapestries, etc. Call or write regarding brochure.

Domestications—P.O. Box 40, Hanover, PA 17333-0040; Telephone: (717) 633-3313.
Mail-order catalog offering a variety of home accessories including curtains, bedding, furnishings, linens, rugs, dinnerware, etc. Call or write for catalog.

Kitschen—15 Christopher Street, New York, NY 10014; Telephone: (212) 727-0430.
Specializes in vintage kitchenware items.

Marston Luce—1314 21st Street NW, Washington, DC 20036; Telephone: (202) 775-9460.
Specializes in outdoor (garden, porch) accessories.

Studio II—P.O. Box 41981, Fredericksburg, VA 22404; Telephone: (703) 786-3242.
Specializes in Victorian lithographs, paintings, etc. Call or write regarding catalog.

Tapestry Inc.—905 Utica-Sellersburg Road, Jeffersonville, IN 47130; Telephone: (812) 288-9045.
Specializes in Victorian tapestry panels, pillows, etc. Call or write regarding brochure.

The Victorian Cupboard—P.O. Box 1852; Old Chelsea Station, New York, NY 10113; Telephone: (800) 653-8033.
Specializes in nineteenth-century specialty foods, sundry items, and antique table and kitchenware items. Call or write for catalog information.

ARCHITECTURAL SALVAGE

Architectural salvage emporiums can be found in most large cities (check local directories) and are a wonderful source for locating vintage hardware, mantels, lighting fixtures, building materials, bathroom furnishings, art-glass windows, garden ornaments, antique furniture, and architectural elements.

Architectural Artifacts, Inc.—4325 North Ravenswood, Chicago, IL 60613; Telephone: (312) 348-0622.

The Brass Knob—2311 18th Street NW, Washington, DC 20009; Telephone: (202) 332-3370.

The Emporium—2515 Morse Street, Houston, TX 77019; Telephone: (713) 528-3803.

Great Gatsby's Auction Gallery—5070 Peachtree Industrial Boulevard, Atlanta, GA 30341; Telephone: (800) 428-7297.

Queen City Architectural Salvage—P.O. Box 16541, Denver, CO 80216; Telephone: (303) 296-0925.

Salvage One—1524 South Sangamon, Chicago, IL 60608; Telephone: (312) 733-0098.

PERIODICALS

Victorian Homes—P.O. Box 61, Miller Falls, MA 0l349.
Published six times a year, including a special holiday issue and a sourcebook issue. A "must have" magazine for the Victorian homeowner or Victoriana enthusiaStreet Published by Vintage Publications, Inc.

Victorian Decorating & Lifestyle—P.O. Box 508, Mount Morris, IL 61054-7995.
Published six times a year by GCR Publishing Group Inc. Magazine focuses on interior decoration and nineteenth-century lifestyles.

Victoria—P.O. Box 7150, Red Oak, Iowa 51591.
A monthly magazine devoted to beauty and fashion, Victorian culture, gardening, travel, etc. Published by the Hearst Corporation.

Photography Credits

©Philip Ennis Photography: Design: Samuel Botero Associates: pp. 116-117, Design: Butlers of Far Hills: pp. 24-25, Design: Carolyn Bronson: p. 92, Design: Anne Cooper Interiors: p. 93, Design: Beverly Ellsley: p. 112, Design: Country Floors: pp. 102, 122, Design: Billy W. Francis Associates: p. 69 right, Design: Patricia Kocak: p. 101, Design: NDM Kitchens: p. 109, Design: Motif Designs: p. 115 bottom left, Design: Barbara Ostrom Associates: pp. 107, 129, 157 bottom right, Design: Tom O'Tool: pp. 84-85, 105, Design: Sharon Pretto Interiors: p. 98, Design: Clifford Stanton: p. 97

©Feliciano: pp. 2, 31, 39 right, 45, 47 top left, 55, 63, 72-73, 89, 160

©Tria Giovan: pp. 29, 46, 50, 120, 121, 132, 134, 137, 142 top left, 153 bottom left, 158-159, 161 bottom left, 162

©Mick Hales: pp. 15, 20, 23, 28, 51, 115 top right, 136, 149

©Nancy Hill: pp. 16, 74, 153 top right, Design: Katie Lee: p. 41

©John Kane: p. 79

©Balthazar Korab: pp. 35, 62, 157 top left

©image/dennis krukowski: Design: Aubergine Interiors, Ltd.: p. 71, Design: Tom Clark: p. 34, Design: David Anthony Easton, Inc.: p. 146, Design: Leta Austin Foster: p. 143, Design:

Irvine & Fleming, Inc.: p. 33, Design: Charles Krewson: p. 87, Design: LEMEAU + LLANA, INC. - LLA-NARTE: p. 83, Design: Tonin MaCallum ASID, Inc.: pp. 8, 19, 125, 133, 138, 161, Design: Ned Marshall, Inc.: p. 141, Design: Mary Meehan Interiors, Inc.: p. 95, Design: Gary Paul Design, Inc.: p. 108, Design: Joseph Pricci, Ltd.: p. 156, Design: Dennis Rolland, Inc.: p. 30

©Keith Scott Morton Photographer: pp. 12, 22, 91 right, 128

©Michael Mundy: Design: Greg Munoz: p. 123, Design: Dennis Rolland Inc.: pp. 42-43, 67, 82, 151, Design: Stingray/Hornsby: p. 37 bottom right

©Peter Paige: p. 85 right

©Robert Perron: Architecture: Robert T. Mudge: p. 124

©David Phelps: pp. 18, 37 top left, 96, 142 bottom right, 145

©Paul Rocheleau: pp. 11, 26, 32, 38-39, 40, 44, 47 bottom right, 52, 56, 65 right, 68-69, 76, 103, 110, 148

©Eric Roth: Design: C. H. Barrett: p. 144, Design: Corol Kaplan: p. 48, Design: Elizabeth Speert Interiors: p. 49, Design: Sugarman: p. 94

©Bill Rothschild: pp. 118, 127

©Ron Solomon/TAB Stock, Inc.: p. 36

©Tim Street-Porter: pp. 27, 126, Design: Tony Duquette: p. 64-65, Design: Ralph Lauren: p. 86

©Brian Vanden Brink: pp. 59, 60, 81, 88, 90-91, 111, 113, 147, 163 right, Design: Robert Currie, Interior Designer: 150

©Vanderschuit/Photo Bank Inc.: p. 152

©Paul Warchol: pp. 114, 131, 154

Photos on pages 15, 20, 28, 51, 136 and 149 were taken at Kingscote historical house courtesy of the Preservation Society of Newport County.

Index